AF531810

IRAQ–2003
THE RETURN OF IMPERIALISM

Zafar Imam

ACADEMY OF THIRD WORLD STUDIES
Jamia Millia Islamia
New Delhi

AAKAR BOOKS
DELHI

IRAQ–2003
The Return of Imperialism

First Published, 2004

ISBN 81-87879-16-5

Published by
AAKAR BOOKS
28-E, Pocket-IV, Mayur Vihar Phase-I, Delhi-110 091
Phone : 22795505 Telefax : 22795641
E-mail : aakarb@del2.vsnl.net.in

Typeset at
Nidhi Laser Point, Shahdara, Delhi-110 032

Printed in India on behalf of M/s Aakar Books by
Arpit Printographers, B-7, Saraswati Complex,
Subhash Chowk, Laxmi Nagar, Delhi-110 092
Ph. : 22825424

CONTENTS

FOREWORD

This book tells one of the most tragic true stories of our own time. A true story, a kind of magic realism, because US invasion of Iraq and its occupation is a ground reality in 2003; while this reality itself is woven round the fantasy of uncovering weapons of mass destruction (WMD) concealed by Iraq and of making Iraq safe for democracy and freedom. A tragic story, because a civil and amply affluent society of our age has destroyed wantonly in a medieval fashion an ancient humankind civilization, deprived and fractured ever since August 1990.

After this demolition job, rather well done, the fantasy of US Establishment has collapsed and its deception exposed, but the truth comes out. The truth is that the USA has practised characteristically 'might is right' in Iraq and it has sought to make huge profits from the miseries of Iraqis. Unbelievable as it is, the imperialists have returned to Baghdad in the year 2003. How soon and how not too soon these new imperialists will pack up and leave, we cannot say. The question, however, before us today, is how to cope with them – the USA and its hangers-on.

Readers are facilitated by presenting this book in a capsular format in an academic framework. A relevant UN document is appended here and resource readings are included.

In writing this book, I have relied upon excellent collection of the library of Third World Academy, Jamia Millia Islamia. I thank the Academy where I have now the privilege of association as a Visiting Professor after my superannuation from Jawaharlal Nehru University.

I hope that this book succeeds in communicating with its readers. Needless to add that I, alone, am responsible for what is said in the book.

New Delhi
31 August, 2003

Zafar Imam

1

IRAQ IN HISTORY

Early History

One of the earliest river valley human settlements lies in between and around the rivers Tigris and Euphrates. In the middle east this river valley civilization was perhaps older than Egypt's Nile valley civilization, though it hardly showed a kind of unity and continuity of Egyptian milieu. Unlike Egypt, the land between Tigris and Euphrate rivers attracted different peoples, speaking diverse languages in south, centre and the north. They were known by a number of names—Sumer and Akkad, Assyria and Babylonia. The Greeks-Romans called it Mesopotamia and the Hebrew Bible, *Aram Naharayim* (Aram of the Two Rivers).

In the pre-Christian era, roughly in 5th Century BC, Babylon turned into a powerful kingdom of distinctive civilization. The king of Babylon, Nebuchadnezzar, captured Jerusalem after subduing the kingdom of Judah, known as Israel. He destroyed the great Jewish temple and exiled its people to Babylon in captivity. A few decades later, Cyrus, the Mede, the founder of a new Persian (later Sasanid) empire, vanquished Babylon and sent back the Jewish exiles home. He also rebuilt the Jewish temple at Jerusalem.[1] As a result, the Euphrates valley became a part of Sasanid empire; so much

1. Thus was founded the historical amity between the Jews and Persians (Iranian) lasting perhaps till now, twentyfirst century.

so that it had built its capital at Ctesiphon near to the site of the present day Baghdad. The name Baghdad is itself Persian and means "Given by God". It was the name of a village, where, later in eighth century, 782 AD, the second Abbasid Arab Caliph, al Mansur, established a new caliphate capital. He named it the "City of Peace", but the name stuck was Baghdad. However, the entire territory was one of the main arenas of friction and war between the two great empires of the time, the Sasanid and the Roman. Northern part of Mesopotamia was particularly hard hit, sometimes ruled by Rome and sometimes by Persia.

When Islam came on the scene in the area, a few years after the death of Prophet Mohammad in 632, Mesopotamia was firmly under Byzantine control with a Christian majority and sprinkle of Jews. In 636 the Arabs under the second Caliph, Umar seized the entire territory including present day Syria and Jerusalem after defeating a huge Byzantine army at Yarmuk Valley (east of present sea of Galilee). In fact, this was the first expansion of Islam, while the turn of Persia, under the Sasanids, came a year later in 637. The name Iraq gradually became current in Arab usage probably under the early Caliphs in the seventh century.

Here it may be pointed out that Mesopotamia was not as important as present-day Syria and other borderlands of Arabian peninsula for example Yemen, for East-West trade, particularly import of silk from China and spices from India to the Mediterranean world. Whatever little importance it could command, it had began to lose when east-west trade through the Arab lands began to decline from third century onwards as a result of almost continuous wars between the Byzantines and Sasanids. Mesopotamia thus remained an epicentre of conflicts, and wars between the two empires of the time, the Sasanid and the Byzantine.

Islam Comes to Iraq

The entry of Arab Islam in Mesopotamia and adjoining region, particularly Persia, was welcome to its population. For one thing, it brought them relief from continuous and uninterrupted Byzantine-Sasanid wars. On the other hand, their economic plight turned much better as a consequence of their conversion to Islam and due to protection of Islam for non-muslims. During the early Caliphate, the administration of newly acquired lands was usually carried out from newly established garrison towns on the edge of deserts or inhabited lands, but where such towns already existed they were used. The territory of Mesopotamia was governed from nearby Damascus, although new garrison towns were established in frontier areas. Kofa and Basra were such new towns in Mesopotamia (Iraq).

Kofa and Basra played a decisive historical role in early Islam. The fourth Caliph, Ali ibn Abu Talib, the cousin and son-in-law of Prophet Mohammad, had developed a strong foot-hold in Kofa. In 657, he had decisively defeated his opponents to Caliphate in the "Battle of Camels", which indeed may be viewed as Islam's "first civil war of succession". After Ali's demise the centre of political Islam shifted to Damascus with the inauguration of Umayyad Caliphate. But Iraq turned into a main base of opposition to Umayyad Caliph Muawiya. This tussle led to Islam's second civil war of succession (680-692) which finally led to the brutal massacre of Prophet's grandson, al Husain at Karbala in 680 by Umayyad troops. Thus began the great schism in Islam, between Shias, supporters of Ali and his son Husain, and Sunnis (their opposite camp). Basra and Kofa continued to lead this civil war for almost two decades; and Shias established themselves in various parts of Arabia, Iran and Iraq. It was only by 692 that Damascus could bring them under its control after ruthless suppression.

Iraq, certainly its central and southern part, emerged as the focal point in Islam within decades after Prophet Mohammad. It was, therefore, no surprise that the succeeding Caliph decided to shift their capital from Damascus to a place on Tigris where it flew closest to its sister river, Euphrates. The place was Baghdad. Baghdad was soon transformed from a small unknown cluster of villages into a famous capital, city of palaces, mosques and gardens. The second Abbasid Caliph, the founder and builder of the Capital-city of Baghdad, took up residence in his new capital in 763 A.D. During the next five hundred years of Abbasid Caliphate, Baghdad grew into a nerve centre of Islamic world. Many of the illustrious men, ideas, movements and architectural stuctures of medieval Islam, indeed human civilization, had originated and prospered in Baghdad and spread from it far and wide.

The Caliphate as an institution soon began to crumble under its own weight. A major offshoot of the weakness of Abbasid Caliphate during the second millenium was emergence of local/regional centres of power. One such centre was in Northern Iraq among the Kurds. It was a Kurd, Salah-al-Din, who went down in the history of Islam as the leader who restored Jerusalem from the crusaders in 1187 to Muslims.

Finally, the hordes of Mongols beseiged the city, and it reluctantly capitulated. Yet the invaders brutally sacked and levelled it to the ground in 1258. However, the invaders soon left the city to fend for itself. Thus was ravished savagely by sheer force a humankind civilization. No wonder that Arab-Islamic power could hardly ever fully recover after that.

After 1258, Iraq became an outlying frontier province and fell prey to vicissitude and waywardness of Bedouin and cut off from outside world. It could no longer serve as the channel of east-west trade. Iraq was thus turned into the fallen city of Caliphs left to centuries of neglect and stagnation.

Meanwhile, the Turks from northern steppes, the Turks of Seljuk dynasty had already appeared in Baghdad towards the middle of tenth century and virtually controlled the Abbasid Caliphs for about a century. Hence, the sack of Baghdad provided them an opportunity. After complicated manoeuvres and some military skirmishes, by the end of 13th century, they had incorporated the local chieftains of Iraq into their empire in central and eastern Anatolia based in the city of Konya. Their rule was brought to an end by a fresh wave of Mongol invasion under Taimur towards the penultimate years of fourteenth century. He annexed Iraq. However, after his death, the Turks resumed their onward journey. By the close of fourteenth century, Baghdad and Iraq were firmly held by Turks under the leadership of the Ottomans.

By the end of fourteenth century, Iraq had thus lost its pivotal position in Islamic world. Its epicentre had shifted to

Mamluks in Egypt and later to Ottoman Turks in Anatolia (Turkey) from 1446 onwards.

Modern History

From early sixteenth century, the Ottoman Turks began their ascendancy in Arab lands, including Iraq. However, conflict and rivalry with their neighbours, Safavid Iran, continued in the region particularly in central-south Iraq, Syria and in the Gulf region. In 1501, Shah Ismail founded the Safavid dynasty in Iran and declared shiism, an offshoot of Islam, as the official creed of Iran. He quickly brought central and south Iraq under his control. However, the Ottomans launched their first war with Safavid Iran in 1514 and the series of war, continued with short interruption of peace until the end of nineteenth century. The Ottomans quickly gained lordship over Sheriff of Mecca, and conquered Syria and Egypt. They took Baghdad and Iraq from Iran in 1534. Two decades later, the Iranians, retook Baghdad. Finally, in 1639, the Ottomans conquered whole of Iraq and it soon became a *vilayat* (province) of Ottoman empire until its very dissolution after the First World War.

For about four centuries, the Ottomans treated Iraq as a rich agricultural belt of their empire and ruled through Governor appointed by them. The Arab population, broadly speaking, were left to themselves.

Interestingly, towards the end of nineteenth century, oil was found in Iraq but the Ottomans did not pay attention to it. On the other hand, the first drilling of oil had already taken place in Russian controlled Azerbaijan as far back as in 1842. The first oil refinery was built in 1863 in Baku. The oilfields developed in Baku roughly in the same period as in Pennsylvania in the USA. Iranian controlled areas had begun drilling oil fields in 1908 at Masjid-e-Sulaiman. Iraq came in the oil production and sale scene later when the Ottomans had begun losing out to Britain and France. The age of extracting oil concessions from middle-east by western businessmen began at the beginning of 20th century when Knox D'Arcy, a British-New Zealander businessman, got concession from the Iranian monarch, a development which finally led to the establishment of Anglo-Persian (later Anglo-Iranian) Oil Company.

From later half of seventeenth century onwards, when the Ottomans were decisively defeated at the gates of the city of Vienna, their empire was on decline. We need not go into details of various complex reasons for its decline. Backwardness of Ottoman society in science and technology, its growing economic weakness and determined policy of western powers for liquidating the Ottoman power in pursuit of their own brand of imperialist expansion, all combined to the decay of the Ottomans.

Iraq as a province *(vilayat)* and hinterland of the empire had also its share of sufferings. Like Syria and Egypt, Iraq registered a rapid decline in population, especially in villages.[2] Once fertile agricultural lands of Iraq river valley were stagnated due to neglect and replacement of military grant system *(Iqta)* with tax farming. Besides, the Ottoman trade with the west had sharply declined from nineteenth century onwards and the handicraft industry of Iraq was hardly hit, in particular. Iraq had by the end of eighteenth century also lost its importance for Ottoman controlled land trade because new sea-routes had opened through Black Sea and Suez Canal.

Among Arab lands of Ottoman empire, Hejaz remained important for outside world because of annual Haj pilgrimage to Mecca and Medina, and the Ottomans kept it that way. However, Iraq, like all other Ottoman-Arab lands, was nothing more than a backyard of the Ottoman empire and it was in deep slumber.

Generally speaking, the Arabs accepted Ottoman rule over their lands. There were some minor exceptions where Ottoman armies were used in force. One frequent occurance from eighteenth century onwards was the ambitious Pashas (governors) seeking to carve out their own rule profiting by the weakness of and disarry of the empire and by the rivalry between Ottomans and Iranians. However, they operated in

---

2. See, Bernard Lewis (1997) *The Middle East: A Brief History of the Last 2000 Years*, Touchstone Edition, New York, pp. 27-28.

Arab lands, including a few in Iraq, but they were not themselves Arabs. Mostly, these rebellions were crushed with a few notable exceptions. Like the one was the case of Mohammad Ali Pasha who succeeded in founding a dynasty ruling a quasi-independent State in Egypt. The other was in northern Lebanon where Druze managed to gain considerable autonomy in the mountains with Christian help. In the Gulf borderlands, a tiny principality, Kuwait managed to gain considerable autonomy around 1756 with a helping hand from Britain. Moreover, the last Ottoman-Iranian war, fought in 1821-23, had stabilized the eastern frontier between the two empires, thereby ending the possibilities of movement for autonomy at eastern borders.

However, serious rebellions led by the Wahhabis took place in Arab land itself, in Hejaz from mid-eighteenth century onwards. But Wahhabi rebellion was essentially a movement for religious puritanism and the Ottoman army increasingly using artillery easily crushed it. Yet the Wahhabi movement did not completely die down and it played an important role in Arab revolt in 1916.

The Arab revolt against the Turks began in the midst of the First World War. It was in the main prompted by the greed and grab of Sharif Husain, the ruler of Hejaz which included the holy cities of Mecca and Medina. On the other hand, it was carefully encouraged and planned by the British during the First World War with a mixture of objectives of defeating the Turks and imperialist expansion. The revolt in Hejaz was half-heartedly dealt by the local Ottoman garrison, while British forces from Egypt began to advance on Palestine. Another British force led by General Allenby occupied Baghdad in April 1917 and later Damascus. By October 1918 when the war ended, Iraq was controlled and occupied by British forces. There thus began the imperialist hold of Iraq.

The method adopted, however, was different than the old classical colonial rule of direct rule and plunder—Britain's rule came over Iraq under a mandate system of the then League of Nations. The proclaimed idea was to prepare Iraq and its people for independence and governing on British model. Besides Iraq, Palestine was also assigned to Britain. Under the same system and with similar objectives France was assigned Syria and Lebanon. The British further split Palestine into two. One was formed an Arab emirate, ruled by Abdullah, another son of Sharif of Hejaz, and called Transjordan (Jordan), while the other was Palestine, kept under direct British administration.

The entire fertile region of the Gulf, including Iraq, thus became the domain of western powers, Britain and France, in a new way, the League of Nations system of mandate.

In pursuance of its imperialist aims the British in 1932, finally installed Faisal, a son of Sharif Husain of Hejaz, as king. The British then declared Iraq as "an independent country with a Westminster type of constitutional monarchy."

It is worthwhile to note that similar developments were taking place all over the middle east. The western colonialisation had staged a comeback, reinforced by legal concessions and agreements to extract, process and market the new wealth of middle-east-oil.

Subsequent events clearly showed that Arab nationalism, unlike in the long spell of Ottoman rule, had begun to protest and organize against the west even during the war time. In despair, it even sought the help of Nazi Germany. In April 1941 a small-time Iraqi politician, Rashid Ali-al-Gaylani, with military support, seized power in Baghdad. His short-lived regime openly favoured the Axis powers. The British within months, overthrew Rashid Ali and installed the puppet king Faisal once again, while Nurial-Said emerged as a strong pro-Britain Prime Minister. Interestingly, in neighbouring Syria, a committee was formed with the object of mobilizing support for Rashid Ali. This was the committee from which sprang the Baath Party, later to split in rival Iraqi and Syrian factions.

In neighbouring Palestine, the mandate system was over. A new state in Palestine, Israel, was brought into existence. With the birth of Israel, Arab nations, took a new turn and generally became much more suspicious of the west (now America) because of its overtly pro-Israeli policies.

It was under these circumstances that by mid-fifties Britain and USA had formally dragged Iraq into their global strategy against the erstwhile Soviet Union. Along with Turkey, Iran and Pakistan, Iraq was made to join a cold war military alliance, the Baghdad Pact, in 1955. Such a move was obviously against the then rising tide of Arab nationalism. A military coup d'etat soon followed. In July, 1958 monarchy was overthrown and a republic was proclaimed. Thereafter began a fresh chapter in the history of modern Iraq.

2

HOW THE WEST CAME

The region, middle-east, has an ancient civilization like India and China. Its strategic location, mid-way between the Mediterranean world and the Eastern world, commanded land routes and sea-lanes for trade, commerce and human intercourse. Human settlements grew round the great rivers of the region; fertile agricultural lands and mineral resources proved decisive. Besides, the region was original source of three major religions—Judaism, Christianity and Islam. For these very reasons, though propensity of ancient kingdoms for wars of conquest and domination was no less important, from times immemorial, outside powers were attracted to the region of middle-east. This process has continued with some interruptions and varied intensity, even now, in the 21st century. Rich oil deposits of the region as well as their cheap extraction and export, turned it into a major, perhaps the most important, source of energy for world economy, hence an added attraction for outside powers.

Historically, the outside powers always came, saw and conquered the middle-east and drew immense advantages to themselves. As a matter of fact, the role of outside powers invariably brought more than usual misery and suffering to the people and habitat of the region, while benefits were far less than satisfactory.

Before the Christian era, the Greeks led by Alexander of Macedonia had conquered it in 356-323 BC and had established Greek rule in Iraq, Iran, Syria and Egypt for about next hundred years. In 64 BC Roman General Pompey conquered Syria, the fertile crescent, and Jerusalem. Only two local or middle-east formations, the Iranians and Jews, could resist the outsiders though unsuccessfully with disastrous results. However, the Iranians somehow continued their struggle against the Greek-Roman domination until 637 when Caliph Umar put an end to their imperial pretensions.

As a matter of fact, the Greek-Romans had begun retreating from the fertile crescent and Jerusalem a year earlier in 636, forced by army of believers. They had now withdrawn to the outer perimeters of their empire in and around their great city of Constantinople. A new chapter in the history of outside interference had begun in the middle-east. The dominant indegenious power of the region, Arab-Islam now expanded outside.

For about the next three hundred and fifty years, Muslim Arabs from Arabia and middle-east had moved mainly in present day Central Asia, Asia Minor, Egypt and north Africa and even in Western parts of India. They even crossed the mediterranean and penetrated into Spain right to the western borders with France. However, the entry of outside powers from Europe was resumed by 1096 when the era of crusades commenced with the arrival of European armies in middle and near east, finally leading to the seizure of Jerusalem from the Arabs in 1099. Since then, in all, about ten crusades were fought for about next six centuries (1686) in two phases. Although the long drawn-out crusades remained inconclusive, at the beginning the Muslims had an upper hand, notwithstanding reverses, but later the European Christians were better placed. In the first phase upto thirteenth century the military struggle was mainly directed against the Arab power and later it was mainly directed against the Ottoman power. It resulted in the gradual withdrawal of outside powers from middle east, capture of Constantinople by the Ottomans in 1453 and to the expansion of Ottoman power to the Balkans, Hungary at the expense of Astro-Hungarian empire. The second phase began when the Ottomans were defeated at the gates of Vienna in January 1683 and as a sequence they were forced to roll back from Europe. Eventually by the end of nineteenth century, their empire was threatened to the verge of collapse.

Indeed by the later part of the eighteenth century, the balance of power had changed in favour of European powers. Apart from traditional rivals, Britain, France and Germany, new outside powers, the Austro-Hungarian and Czarist empires had entered into the fray. The way to the middle-east was forced open as the Ottoman empire began to disintegrate. The beginning of first World War in 1914 and the defeat of the Ottoman finally brought the outside powers right in the near and middle-east.

This is thus not difficult to understand that the penetration of outside powers in the region of middle and near east and their growing influence, both were made possible by the very process of decline of Ottoman empire. An empire being replaced in the region gradually and in stages by yet another one, the stronger, if not better one. Let us look at this very process more intently.

The West in the Middle-East

It is now generally recognised that economic position, particularly commerce and trade, of the Islamic middle-east during the high middle ages was far advanced in every way than that of Europe. It was richer, larger, better organised with more commodities to sell and more money to buy, and a fairly sophisticated network of trading relations. By the end of the middle-ages, roughly by the close of the seventeenth century, these positions were reversed.

There were of course many domestic factors in Islamic middle-east in its decline, for instance, militarization of the Ottoman empire and the hold of military autocracy over it with little concern for socio-economic development. Among the external factors, rapid pace of scientific and technological advancement in Europe and its enrichment by colonization of America, were crucial. This is a complicated and long story, and as such this need not detain us. Suffice here to summarize, in the words of Bernard Lewis, a noted western authority on the middle-east: "Ottoman armies ruled the land and Ottoman fleets for a while dominated the seas; but the European merchants, quietly and peacefully captured the market".

After the defeat of the Ottoman empire at the gates of Vienna in 1683, it was the Christian Europe that advanced from strength to strength, while the Islamic middle-east suffered loss of power and muscle. Gradually, the Ottomans were thrown out of Europe and back to their confines in Asia. Even their capital, Istanbul, and its environment were threatened a number of times by European powers from the west and Czarist Russia from North. In a classic model of the beginning and expansion of modern colonialism, here too, trade followed the flag. The rise of mercantalism in Europe from seventeenth century resulted in expansion of trade and formation of trading companies. These trading companies were protected, encouraged and helped by European governments. On the other hand, the Ottomans were down militarily, and they were incapacitated even to regulate their activities. The western trading companies thus found it easier to penetrate in the middle-east. Even the traditional superiority of middle-east in the export of manufactured textiles to the west was put in the reverse gear from Europe to middle east. Symbolically, coffee and sugar, already widely used in the middle-east from mid-seventeenth century onwards, came from Europe. Initial trading activity soon gave way to economic penetration, then domination, and, finally political control. For a start, a number of ways and means were adopted. Unlike the export of middle-east products to the west, which was restricted and in some cases excluded by protective tarrifs, western export and trade to middle-east were sheltered by the capitulation system. In fact, the capitulation system ensured the right of goods in a foreign country/domain. Ottoman, Persian and other Muslim rulers granted this privilege to Christian states allowing their citizens to reside and trade in their domains without any fiscal and other liabilities imposed by them on their own non-Muslim subjects. Thus such privileges were granted to Italian maritime states in the fourteenth and fifteenth centuries, to France in 1569 and to England in 1580.[1] As the Ottoman and Persian empires weakened steadily, these trading privileges far

1. Bernard Lewis (1997), *op.cit.*, p. 291.

exceeded than those originally intended. By late eighteenth century, European diplomatic missions assumed the practice of granting on their own directly these privileges, now vastly extended. The Europeans and minorities, like Jews, Greeks and Armenian, almost completely dominated over the financial matters of Ottoman domain by the beginning of twentieth century. In this game, the Russians had also joined, after the imposed treaty of Kücük Kaynarca in 1774 on the Ottomans and established a virtual protectorate over orthodox Christian communities of the empire in Balkans, Anatolia and in Syria, then all provinces of Ottoman empire. All these privileges and protections were freely exercised and administered by respective embassies and consulates. Economic domination of foreigners and Christian and Jewish minorities thus extended to almost all spheres of life in Ottoman societies and their hold on them thus grew over the years.

Like colonialism such foreign domination over Ottomans did bring about some positive changes, like modern education, communication and new ideas. A major change was noticeable in modernization of Ottoman army and reforms of administration in the middle east, in general.

All these, however, came late to prevent the decline of Muslim powers in middle-east and Iran. By the end of the nineteenth century, the dual process of the military advance of the west and the decline of Ottomans and Iranians had gained momentum. At the beginning of twentieth century, the final plans of war against Ottomans had commenced in Balkans and ended in their total defeat in the First World War. By spring of 1917, British forces had occupied Baghdad in Iraq, and Palestine in December 1917, Damascus in October 1918. On October 30, 1918, the Ottomans signed the surrender documents on a British warship, *Agamemnon* at anchor off Mudros in the island of Lemnos. The Ottomans were forced to retreat from heartland of Arab lands (Hejaz) and were rolled back to Anatolia proper.

By November 1918, middle-east came under direct and total control of the European powers. However, their total control and domination were exercised once again by a characteristic manner of colonialism of 20th century—indirect rule, understood as neo-colonialism. Indeed it may well be argued that the practice of neo-colonialism in contemporary history originated and developed in middle east. It is indeed ironic that the domination and control of west over middle-east also began to be viewed in religious terms—retreat and defeat of Islam by advance and victory of Christianity. However, the idea of crusades—the clash of civilizations—was yet to be given a new lease of life at the end of twentieth century and the beginning of twentyfirst century.

The West in IraqL: Eighteenth Century and After

As we have pointed out in Chapter one, during the Ottoman rule the entire region of present day Iraq was administered like a *vilayat* (province) with considerable autonomy to its governors. This autonomy increased in direct proportion to the weakening of Ottoman administration, centralised at Istanbul.

Unlike other constituents of the Ottoman empire, this region, except the coastal-area of the Gulf, however attracted little European attention. Initially, until the end of eighteenth century the Dutch were dominant power in Gulf coastal area. In 1763 only Basra was the centre of British trade and an agency of East India Company was established there. Baghdad itself had still not risen after the demolition of the Mongols and later adventures of warring clans. But after Napolean had reached Egypt in 1789, Britain became active in Iraq and swiftly replaced the Dutch. In 1798, a permanent British resident was appointed in Baghdad. The growth of telegraphic communication and the need for ensuring the safety and security of Britain's growing Indian empire was prime consideration for the British at the end of eighteenth century. It was, therefore, logical that British interests were looked after from the office of Governor-General in India and through it from London. Britain's involvement in Iraq thus originated and developed out of its colonial expansion and acquisition.

Immediately after the surrender of Ottoman army following the armistice of Mudros, the invading British army occupied Iraq and administered it. Britain formalised this arrangement in 1920 after the newly established League of

Nations awarded it a mandate over Iraq under its mandatory system.

However, British mandate over Iraq sparked off fierce opposition by various Iraqi tribes and clans and shia mujtahids (preachers). British government suppressed these by brute force under the direction of British High Commissioner, Sir Percy Cox. The British quickly learnt a lesson and proceeded to try other means. A son of Sharif Husain of Mecca was made the king in August after the British-managed referendum approved his accession. Britain further kept its pretence of promoting democracy in Iraq after it made the new king Faisal sign a 25 years Anglo-Iraqi agreement in 1930 so as to continue its presence in the region. It took further precaution by carving out of Iraq a small separate state on the gulf coasts with rich oil deposits, Kuwait and put Sheikh Sabah, another son of Sharif of Mecca, and brother of Iraqi king, as its Emir. Only then Britain declared Iraq as constitutional monarchy on British pattern, withdrew its formal mandate and proclaimed Iraq as an independent State in 1930. It was also ironical that when the League of Nations was already on its way out, Iraq was made its member.

Unfortunately, the Iraqis never accepted British 'experiment in democracy' in Iraq. No sooner than king Faisal died in 1933 that Iraq was rocked by uprisings, internal strifes and anti-British agitations. Inspite of military support from the British, the new king was overthrown by a coup d'etat, engineered by Iraqi army. The king was restored after British intervention but he faced about seven military coups during 1936-41. The tradition of intervention in politics by Iraqi army was thus a direct consequence of Britain's domination over Iraq.

Meanwhile, the Second World War had begun. Nazi Germany found an ally in a section of vocal anti-British intelligentsia and military officers. It was in this phase of Iraqi nationalism that the Baath party was formed and a pro-Nazi regime, led by Rashid Ali al-Gaylani took over power. The British army once again openly intervened and Rashid Ali was killed in encounter and a pro-British Prime Minister, Nuri al-Said was installed in 1942.

Nuri al-Said was a thorough bred Anglophile politician, who outdid the British in seeking to suppress dissent and protest of Iraqis. Immediately after the war, student demonstrations and industrial unrest become consistently recurrent. The more Nuri al-Said repressed them, the more widespread they became. This was also the time when oil production in Iraq had registered a quantam jump, while Arab lands came under the spell of Arab nationalism and Arab unity, espoused by Egypt's Nasser.

It was in this surcharged environment that British committed the blunder of drawing Iraq to the system of US sponsored military alliances against the former Soviet bloc. In 1955, Iraq was pressurised in formally joining the Baghdad Pact along with, Britain, Turkey and Pakistan with the USA backdriving.

Nuri al-Said was rather hell-bent on throwing challenges to the rising tide of Arab nationalism which had surged in Iraq as well. His government showed considerable reluctance in supporting Nasser in the Suez crisis of 1956. In fact, he took the side of the British under the pretext of Anglo-Iraqi agreement of 1930, renewed later. Moreover, in early 1950s, Iraqi oil production had registered yet another quantum jump, though the revenues were channelled to British economic interests rather to economic advancement of Iraq. This drain out of Iraqi economy further ignited discontent and unrest. On top of all, as a response to the merger of Egypt and Syria into a United Arab Republic in 1958, Iraq and Jordan formed a federation under a common Hashemite crown (the grandfather of both kings of Iraq and Jordan was one and the same, Hussain, the Sharif of Mecca who had rebelled against the Ottomans during the First World War under a carefully crafted British plan). This development was like the proverbial last nail in the coffin of the Iraqi regime. Within weeks, in July 1958, it was ousted by Iraqi military, in a coup d'etat.

The military take-over was engineered by a small group of nationalist minded top army officers, led by Brigadier Abdul Karim Qasim. The new government was an uneasy coalition of army officers and nationalist individuals. But it did manage to launch on its agenda quickly. It withdrew from Baghdad

Pact and sterling area, declared non-alignment in foreign policy and came close to the then Socialist bloc. It did appear that the British had lost the game finally in the middle-east and the USA was now fast moving in to fill this vacuum. The Qasim regime struggled to survive against heavy odds internally, from factional disunity and externally, from continued pressure on its borders through US armed incursions in seas near Syria and Lebanon, while other client states in the region like Saudi Arabia and monarchist Iran were also activated. A number of coups followed from September 1959 to February 1963, when plotters eventually succeded in killing Qasim and taking over power.

The post-Qasim years in the history of modern Iraq, February 1963 to July 1968, about five and a half years, are littered with military coups and untold violence against Iraqi communists and their sympathisers. So much so that within two weeks, of 17 July and 30 July 1968, there were two coups. It was in 30 July 1968 coup that Saddam Husain emerged as the sole leader of Baath party and Vice-President of Iraqi Republic. During these years Baath party was proscribed by successive Iraqi governments but it remained active.

It was probably the growing pressure of Baath party and Nasserite nationalists that even during these interregnum years, February 1963–July 1968, successive Iraqi governments continued to stick to the agenda set by Qasim government, that is to say, Revolutionary Command Council (RCC), earlier. The implementation of the programme got accelerated from 30 July 1968 when Saddam Husain assumed the leadership.

The ruling Revolutionary Command Council (RCC) nationalised foreign owned Iraq Oil Company, IOC in 1972, while the role of state sector in economy grew to near monopoly. Oil price increase of 1970s did also help, while Iraq was one of the founder members of OPEC. Saddam oversaw rapid strides in wiping out illiteracy, improvement in social services, and above all, in developing infrastructure for industrialization, arm manufacturing, petro-chemical and iron and steel complexes and thermal power generation. Iraqi economy continued to grow rapidly despite Israeli air strike in June 1981 on its experimental nuclear reactor.

More importantly, Saddam began dealing with restive Kurds in early seventies by granting them autonomy on erstwhile Yugoslav model. By 1974-75, the Kurds, however, wanted more autonomy and they staged insurrection in northern Iraq with an overt support of Shah of Iran. Saddam was instrumental in crushing these by force. On July 16, 1979, Saddam formally took over as President of the republic in the wake of Islamic revolution in Iran.

As relations with Islamic Republic of Iran deteriorated, Saddam came closer to USA; this coincided when the USA equally felt threatened by new Iran. Iraq launched its war against Iran in 1981 which lasted till 1988.

Soon a bitter local war against Iran was fought with overt support and sustenance from the USA and the west. In November 1984, formal diplomatic relations with the USA were restored which were broken in 1967 as a protest against US support to Israel in the 1967 six-day Arab-Israel war. Iraq also came close to Saudi Arabia, Kuwait and post-Nasser Egypt. However, relations with ex-USSR and other European Socialist countries continued to develop.

Iraq-Iran disastrous conflict brought pragmatism to Saddam Husain. It also brought back the USA in full force in Iraq. Later events were however, to show that neither of the two proved an asset to Saddam's Iraq and its people.

3

ESSENTIALS OF US POLICY

Until the First World War, the USA generally kept itself aloof from the middle east. This had certainly suited the great imperial powers of the day—Britain, France, Czarist Russia and Kaiser's Germany. The defining attraction of the middle-east, Iraq included, for the USA—oil–came much later, from the third decade of twentieth century onwards.

Ironically, US interest in the middle-east originated with Britain's Belfour Declaration of 1917 on a Jewish home in Palestine and Anglo-French plans on the division of Ottoman empire in the middle-east. President Woodrow Wilson felt uneasy as he came to know of the plans more closely during the Versailles Peace Conference in 1919. He sent a commission to the middle-east in 1919, even when Britain and France had declined to co-operate. This was a two-member commission comprising Charles R. Crane, the Chicago millioniare and a friend and Dr. Henry Churchill King. The commission went to the middle-east in 1919, interviewed a cross-section of Arab opinion. The commission reported to the President on one unanimous opinion found among the Arabs of the region against settlement of Jews in Palestine. Later Robert Crane emerged in 1930 as one of the originators of idea of developing US stakes in a possible oil wealth of eastern and northern Arabia. With great devotion to his mission and after complicated manoeuvres he got the then US oil giant, Socal, involved in negotiations with King Abdul Aziz of Arabia for rights of exploration in his kingdom. Abdul Aziz was almost certain that Arabia had no oil and the Americans were wasting their time and money. In any case, his preference was for Britain, but Britain was equally sure of the non-existence of oil in Arabia. Finally, the Americans successfully pursuaded Abdul Aziz to sign a deal in early May 1933.[1] Thereafter the story of US stakes in oil in Saudi Arabia really began; oil started to flow on May 1, 1939.

The USA thus came on the scene later simply because the successive US administrations, certainly upto the beginning of the First World War had considered the middle-east as Britain's sphere of activity and influence. As late as July 1941, President Roosevelt thought that the middle-east was "a little far afield for US."[2]

Indeed in many ways, such US views were then realistic and pragmatic. We have described earlier, how Britain was consistently expanding in the region from seventeenth century onwards at the cost of Ottoman Turkey. By the beginning of twentieth century, Britain had extracted concession from nominally independent Iran for exploration and extraction of Iranian oil for a British businessman, William Knox D'Arcy. Willian Knox was mainly instrumental in creating concessionary company, Anglo Persian (later Iranian) Oil Company. This enterprise drilled its first oil well at Masjid-i-Sulaiman, near the Gulf coast in 1908. Interestingly, as said earlier, oil was discovered in Czarist Russian controlled Iran (Azerbaijan) as far back as in 1842 and the first oil refinery was already built in Baku in 1863. The US oil industry was almost a contemporary of that of Czarist Russia.

Iranian type concession soon followed first in Iraq, then in Saudi Arabia and in other parts. Involved in the process were British, Dutch, American and French oil interests. Thus oil turned into a major attraction for outside powers in the middle-east.

The turn of Iraq came after Iran in 1925, when Anglo-Iranian Oil Company established its subsidiary, Iraq Oil

1. The entire course of negotiation is aptly described relying on contemporary sources in the monumental work on Saudi Arabia; See, Robert Lacey. *The Kingdom,* (1982), Fontana Paperbacks, London, pp. 225-37.
2. *Ibid.*, p. 260.

Company (IOC). It first discovered oil in Kirkuk region of north Iraq in 1927. In 1932 and 1938 IOC gained further concession from British controlled Iraqi government and by the close of 1934 Iraq began to export crude oil. It stepped up its production every year as new facilities were found and established. By early fifties it was exporting 28 million tons.

Meanwhile, Britain had further strengthened its hold on the middle-east oil when its small Gulf coast protectorate, Kuwait began drilling oil wells in its territory in 1936 under British control. The USA was certainly aware of growing British hold on oil in the middle-east. Its interest in the middle-east finally fructified during the final stages of Second World War. One immediate reason was flirtations of Saudi king, Iraqi and other Arab nationalist minded leaders with Nazi Germany. But the primary motive was the so-called energy crises or strategic shortage of oil. By 1943, the USA had realised that during the war, the USA as a main source of energy supply to the allies, was "pumping oil 63 percent of the entire world oil consumption everyday from her own reserves; it was 3.8 millions per day" a little more than a third of Saudi Arabia's 10.3 millions per day in 1931.[3] The experts had calculated that US national oil reserves were dropping at the rate of 3 percent per year.[4]

US policy-makers were worried and search for solution had led them to reinforce the idea of burning foreign oil. Venezuela in South America was obvious traditional choice for them. By 1933, when US companies already had concessions in Saudi Arabia, while the drain of US oil resources during the war had catapulated the middle-east oil to priority. Hence, a policy decision was made to go for the middle-east oil with or without Britain. Lend-lease programme had started generously pouring in Saudi Arabia from 18 February 1943. In February 1945 President Roosevelt played gracious host to the Saudi king at a US warship in Great Bitter lake,[5] and the deal was sealed

3. *Ibid.*, p. 362.
4. *Ibid.*
5. *Ibid.*, pp. 240-71.

within two days. The British were unhappy as they had been financing the Saudi king since he had staged a revolt against the Ottoman rule in 1916-17 at their instigation. The USA had thus came to the middle-east for oil and it certainly intended to stay, come what may. "It is our belief that," recorded a US memorandum of December 1942, "the development of Saudi Arabian petroleum resources should be viewed in the light of broad national interest."[6] From Saudi oil to Iraqi oil was a convenient logical jump after the second World War. Iraq was already known to have the second largest reserves of oil in the region.

By the time second World War ended, the US state department had rightly noted that oil "has historially played a large part in external relations of the United States, than any other commodity."[7] It was noted that the middle-east was "a stupendous source of strategic power and one of greatest material prices in world history."[8]

As the post-Second World War unfolded with growing intensity of cold war, US preoccupation with the middle-east oil also grew. Not that the USA was dependent on import of oil from the middle-east or elsewhere, it had its own oil and gas.

Much cheaper, perhaps of better quality and readily available, was oil from the middle-east. Burning of foreign oil and saving its own reserves became an article of faith in the USA.

According to US government Energy Information Administration (EIA),[9] total US imports of crude oil during the years 1999-2002 had been on an annual average more than double of its domestic production. The share of the middle-east oil in percentage of total imports year-wise was; 27 percent in 1999, 28 percent in 2000, 31 percent in 2001 and 26 percent

---

6. As cited in *Ibid.*, p. 263.
7. Quoted in Anthony Arnove, ed. (2002), *Iraq Under Siege*, First Indian edn., Viva Books Ltd., New Delhi, p. 18.
8. *Ibid.*, p. 71.
9. Statistics taken from *Petroleum Economist*, (London), January 2003, p. 3.

in 2002 (first eight months). Of which, the share of Saudi Arabia/Iraq year-wise was 16 percent/6 percent, 17 percent/ 7 percent, 19 percent/9 percent and 17 percent/6 percent. In other words, annual average share of total US import of crude oil from the middle-east was 29 percent during 1999-2002, while Saudi Arabia's share was 18.5 percent (about 1.5 million barrels per day) and Iraq's 7.5 percent (more than 700,000 barrels per day).

So it is arguable whether the USA really needs the middle east oil or may prefer today alternate sources of oil supply.

However, the entire issue is not as simple as that. One of the perceptive planners and activists of US foreign policy, George Kennan had advanced some plausible explanation as early as 1948 for a basic framework of US middle-east policy. "We have about 50 percent of the world's wealth but only 6.3 percent of its population ...... In this situation, we cannot fail to be the object of envy and resentment. Our real task in the coming period is to devise a pattern of relationships which will permit us to maintain this position of disparity without positive detriment to our national security. To do so, we will have to dispense with all sentimentality and day-dreaming and our attention will have to be concentrated everywhere on our immediate national objectives."[10]

When George Kennan was thus advising the state department, the cold war had begun. Soon, the west had launched its post-Second World War global system of military alliances against Communism. In 1949, NATO was established, while Baghdad Pact and SEATO followed. Going by the war-time experience of "strategic shortage" of US oil reserves, President Truman had accorded top priority to ensuring an uninterrupted flow of the middle-east oil to his European allies, and to his own growing cold war military machine around the globe. Oil from Saudi Arabia was then of course under direct US control through US oil giant *Aramco* with Saudi Arabia getting small cut on its oil under the concession agreement. Saudi oil production kept on increasing and *Aramco* remained in charge. When Saudi oil production had reached

10. *Ibid.*, p. 18.

10.3 million barrels per day in 1980-81 compared to 6.3 million barrels per day in 1975, *Aramco* became a 100 per cent Saudi company by mutual agreement in 1980. But over half of Saudi-Aramco production continued to be earmarked for *Aramco* created management contract corporation, comprising Socal, Exxon, Texaco and Mobil. This management corporate distributed, their share, more than 50 per cent of Saudi oil production among themselves; the rest was at the disposal of Saudi Government through OPEC quota.[11] This arrangement worked and suited all and Saudi petro-dollars continued to be handled by US banks at New York. On top of all, Saudi oil, like Iraqi oil, is of good quality and very cheap to produce. In early eighties, less than 10,000 workers manned the Saudi oil surface facilities; this really meant that, it was estimated, 90 per cent of government revenues were generated by less than 1 per cent of national labour force.[12] Certainly a far cry from similar expensive ventures in Alaska, Texas and North sea.

US and its allies were thus not to feel threatened again by any "strategic shortage" of oil even if the cold war might have gone out of control. However, huge oil reserves in countries like Iraq were alluring.

It was at this stage that the US companies began to show real interest in Iraqi oil. One year before, mandate system had formally ended in Iraq and Britain had granted it *de jure* formal independence in 1930. In 1931, the subsidiary company, Turkish Petroleum Company, was reconstituted into Iraq Petroleum Company (IPC). In the reconstituted IPC, 23.5 percent share each was owned by British, Dutch, French companies and jointly by two US oil corporations; the remaining 6 percent was held by Partex owned by Portugese businessman of Ottoman-Armenian descent, Calouste Gulbenkian, rightly perhaps regarded as father of Iraqi oil.[13] IPC negotiated successfully further concessionary terms with suppliant Iraqi government in 1938 under pressure from Britain.

---

11. Robert Lacey (1982), *op.cit.*, pp. 493-94.
12. *Ibid.*, p. 499.
13. www.gulbenkian.pt

The US companies had thus made a small beginning in Iraqi oil. But oil production in Iraq grew by leaps and bounds and their role also proportionately increased. The quantum jump was registered after the Second World War in 1951.

The US administration was, however, far from satisfied. Alarm bells had rung by Arab oil embargo of 1973, however, ineffective and by sneaking of the Soviet Union in Iraqi oil. By the end of the decade, Iran had also turned hostile. More action was needed for securing access to the middle-east oil.

Earlier, by the turn of the twentieth century, geologists and explorers all over the world were convinced of huge oil reserves stretching from Caspian, through Gulf to Black sea. Various governments had redoubled efforts to extract cheap and unequal concessionary deals for their nationals for drilling and exporting of oil. The British had first succeeded in Iran in 1908 and Anglo-Persian (Iranian) Oil Company was founded. Anglo-Persian Oil Company also established a subsidiary with controlling share after First World War in Iraq, the Turkish Petroleum Company (TPC). Meanwhile, in dividing the territories of the Ottoman empire, the British took care by attaching the oil rich areas of Mosul and Kirkuk in the north with the territory of Iraq in 1921 under its mandatory power of League of Nations. Likewise, it drew the boundaries of new State of Iraq in the south with rich oil bearing gulf region, Kuwait, which in turn was earlier extracted by British from the Ottoman Sultan as autonomous province.

After securing necessary concessionary rights from British controlled Iraq, the Anglo-Persian subsidary company, Turkish Petroleum Company (TPC), soon began looking for oil in northern Iraq. The company finally struck oil in 1927 in the region at Kirkuk.

By early 1970s, there were five companies that dominated the world oil industry; two US based, two primarily UK based and one primarily based in France. US based Exxon Mobil loomed largest in the world. Consequently the USA ranked first in corporate oil sector, UK second and France trailing behind as a distant third.[14] US and UK companies led.

14. Anthony Arnove, ed. (2002), *op.cit.*, p. 97.

At about the same time, road blocks had begun to appear in western drive for the middle-east oil. First, the Iranians took the plunge in 1952 under Mossadeq Government when it tried to get favourable terms in the huge profit of Anglo-Iranian Oil Company. Openly interfering, the then US ambassedor to Tehran, Llyod Henderson, assisted in removing Mossadeq Government. Within weeks in 1953 UK-USA sponsored international oil consortium for 'managing' Iranian oil at their terms. Britain's share in the consortium was reduced from near monopoly to 54 percent, while the remaining share was controlled by US companies, Standard Oil, Vaccum, Socal and others. From that point, US stakes in Iran grew in rapid strides until the Iranian Islamic revolution took control of its oil in 1979.

In Iraq, the issue of foreign control of Iraqi oil had turned live from the very beginning in the thirties, particularly after the sudden death of Britain's chosen king Faisal I in 1933. The foreign companies in Iraq Petroleum Company (IPC) on the other hand, had begun to pressurise the Iraqi government for more concessions and rights of extracting oil from new finds. This was an unpopular issue in Iraq. However, the new king succumbed and signed new concession in 1938 in the midst of military coup d'etats and agitations. A nationalist minded Rashid Ali led a successful revolt and formed an anti-British government in April 1941. In May 1941, the British took military action from its strongholds in Jordan and overthrew Rashid Ali by force and reinstalled the old regime. Iraqi oil remained under British control until July 1958, when Brigadier Abdul Karim Qasim seized power in Iraq.

The post-war oil boom in Iraq had not benefitted the Iraqi people. Whatever little investment in human development was made, it was in long-term invisible projects like building irrigation dams, etc. On the other hand, the surge of Arab nationalism from Nasser's Egypt had swept through students, workers and intelligentsia in Iraq as well.

In this surcharged atmosphere USA and UK prompted Nuri al-Said, an Anglophile prime minister, to bring Iraq under a chain of military pacts and alliances against the former Communist bloc. The joining of the Baghdad Pact by Iraq in

1955 was the proverbial last straw. The government was overthrown and military assumed power under a anti-nationalist dominated leadership in 1958.

The issue of foreign ownership of Iraqi oil was indeed a major domestic issue. Immediately, Brigadier Qasim, the new leader, opened negotiations with shareholders of Iraq Petroleum Company for favourable terms. These were prolonged for two years with increasing impatience of Iraqi nationalists. Finally, in 1961, Qasim issued a decree withdrawing the authority of Iraq Petroleum Company for prospecting oil in new Iraqi lands including the oil rich Rumeila. He also set up a separate oil company, Iraq National Oil Company (INOC) and began negotiations with former Soviet Union for prospecting and refining oil.

The Iraq Petroleum Company with active support of US, British and Dutch Governments challenged the law. The issue dragged on until 1969 when a semblance of compromise was reached. On the other hand, in October 1961, INOC was given exclusive powers and rights to develop Rumeila oil field and soon it set to work with the help of oil industry of erstwhile Soviet Union.

Negotiations with Iraq Petroleum Company had dragged too long without results causing increasing differences on both sides. IPC began using open pressure tactics, like it halved the output of Kirkuk oil fields in March 1972. Finally, the government nationalised the IPC in June 1972. It thus became the first Arab Government to do so, hence the most hated in western corridors of power. Western oil companies had traditionally held three quarters share of huge Iraqi oil production and its revenues, and looked for lucrative new oil fields of Rumeila. As discussed earlier, the nationalization of Iraq Petroleum Company followed in 1972. This was preceded by acrimonous relationship between successive Iraqi governments and the two big US and UK companies. For about a decade Iraq sought to gain greater control of its oil as against determined opposition from foreign oil companies. All this perhaps delayed nationalisation. When it finally came, these US and UK companies, mainly—Exxon Mobil (US) and British Petroleum (UK)—lost a good deal of money and shares. On top of it, President Saddam Husain immediately after nationalization signed contracts with Soviet oil industry and with France in seeking investment partnership, thereby foreclosing the possibility of return of US and UK oil giants to Iraqi oil.

The issue of oil thus turned into the crux of impending crises. But the real road block in the western eyes was sourced by the rising surge of Arab nationalism unleashed by Nasser and by successful nationalization of Suez canal in mid-fifties.

The powerful US and UK oil giants, who had lost great stakes in Iraqi oil, certainly did not keep quiet. They all loved to go back to Iraq and begin all over again.

Meanwhile, Iraq had taken a rearguard action. It had signed in April 1972 a 15 year treaty of friendship and cooperation with the then USSR, which had included commitments of mutual defense in case of aggression. Coming at the height of military power of the then Soviet Union in the seventies and its historic tug of war with the USA, this treaty appeared to have checked the design and influence of US oil cartels in White House for about two decades. It was no other than Saddam himself that provided them excuse in 1990-91 by his rash military annexation of Kuwait.

Suffice here to point out that the resumption of US oil stakes in Iraq and the middle-east, even when it had no rival like the former USSR, was once again put on top of US agenda. In 1999, General Anthony C. Zinni, commander-in-chief of US central command testified before the congress that the Gulf region with it huge oil reserves was a "vital interest of long standing for the USA" and the USA must have free access to the regions resources.[15] Who would ensure "free access" to this vital interests of the USA? Of course, the military might of the one and only super-power, "the hyper-power", as the French say, the USA.

One may pause here to pose the question. What is all this fuss about the middle-east oil, if the running and development of US economy and its needs were not really dependent on it

15. *Ibid.*, p. 96.

or on cheap middle-east oil import. The UK, Japan and Western Europe are dependent on it. But with new finds in Alaska and elsewhere, the western oil reserves may even outlive world's largest oil reserves of today in Saudi Arabia and Iraq, put together.

Economists would provide answers to our poser in a number of computerised versions. But one fact has to be common for their validity—middle-east oil income deposited in New York's Manhattan banks, keeps in lubricating world financial market. Just one example should suffice here. In 1981, Saudi Arabia Monetary Agency (SAMA), responsible agency for Saudi investment, was reported to have 100 billion US dollars currency reserves in Manhattan banks. These reserves after budgeted expenditure were built up by $ 300 million worth of sale of oil everyday on the dot; that was in 1981.[16] Then in 2003 all this may safely be guessed to be more than double. Such safe reserves surely add, not diminish, the strength and potential of US economy worldwide. Rivalry among the US and Western powers for controlling and overseeing the middle-east oil has never died down, rather it has of late increased. New entrants like Russia's oil giants, Lukoil have entered in the game in the late nineties. Besides, the cutting off profitable positions of the US and UK oil giants, occupied in Iraqi oil industry since its inception, by nationalization of Iraq Oil Company (IPC) had angered them. Further, this has increased their apprehension that the Russian and French oil conglomerates might step in oil market in Iraq firmly and replace them eventually.

So one can easily find the reason dë'tre of ongoing US-UK military onslaught on Iraq. Likewise, its real objectives behind the publicised noble ones come out. Writing in 1995, a perceptive and well-informed scholar of the middle-east, Bernard Lewis, was still arguing, like any other western scholar of mid-twentieth century, on the objectives of western policy in the region.

"The countries of the outside world-that is to say, of Europe,

16. Robert Lacey (1982), *op.cit.*, p. 474.

America and increasingly, of the Far East—were basically concerned with three things in the middle east; a rich and growing market for their goods and services, a major source of their energy needs, and, as a necessary means to safeguarding the first two, the maintenance of atleast some semblence of international law and order."[17]

How true, even now, after US-UK ongoing war on Iraq began from March 2003!

17. Bernard Lewis (1997), *op.cit.*, p. 386.

4

US POLICY IN ACTION

A major impact of the disintegration of the Soviet Union in December 1991 was the growing readiness of the US as a lone superpower to go to war for the maintainance of regional and global 'stability' conducive to its own economic and strategic interests. Such a hot pursuit of 'international stability' has of late become a self-proclaimed US responsibility. This has also become an important goal of US foreign policy today with least consideration for the United Nations as well as with utter disregard for international law. Hence, US military power must always be in harness; and US political leadership must demonstrate its willingness to employ it in more than one spheres anywhere, anytime. Any opposition, big or small, ongoing or potential, must be contained, or if not, must be demolished by force through regime change, upholding the right of intervention. Action must be taken without delay and hesitation as, in the words of Dick Cheney, the US vice-president, "the risk of inaction is far greater than the risk of action". It was certainly for nothing that during the 1991 Gulf war, former US President, Bush I bluntly declared "what we say goes".[1]

According to US Constitution, it is only the Congress which can declare war. This constitutional right it has exercised five times so far; 1812 (against Britain), 1845 (against Mexico), 1898 (against Spain), 1916 (World War I) and 1942 (World War II).

1. As cited in Noam Chomsky, *"US-Iraq Policy: Motives and Consequences"*, in Anthony Arnove, ed. (2002), *op.cit.*, p. 72.

In the wake of terrorist attack on the USA in September 2001, a unanimous resolution of the Congress gave wide powers to President George W. Bush (Bush II) to fight against terrorism; it, however, did not constitutionally declare war.

These constitutional niceties apart, US presidents have sent US troops abroad at least 120 times.[2] The troops must be withdrawn within ninety days untill the congress approves it. In January 1991, President George Bush (I) got congressional approval for Gulf operations by a narrow margin of only 3 votes in the US senate.[3]

Looking at the record of US foreign policy, this does appear that the use of force has remained a main instrument of US foreign policy.[4] Rhetorics on freedom, democracy and noble ideals of founding fathers notwithstanding, US presidents have not in the past hesitated in actually employing military might of the USA in pursuit of proclaimed US objectives of the time. On the other hand, the threat to use force was unabashfully reiterated time and again. The economic might of the USA is another portent instrument of US foreign policy. Linking of economic ties or foreign aid with the objectives of US foreign policy anywhere at a given time has been an article of faith for US policy makers. Its latest example was Yemen, a poor nation in Arab world, whose long-term development aid was cut down, even cancelled, when it did not vote for use of force in Iraq in the UN Security Council (first Gulf war) in 1991 (Resolution 678). Such examples abound, hence these need not detain us here.

During the cold war era, these portent instruments were, however, generally not employed as a practice. More importantly, collective sanction of the UN, as for instance, the Korean War, was sought after, while respect of international law was usually kept in mind. The disintegration of the USSR and the consequent status of the USA as the lone mighty

---

2. Dilip Hiro. *Iraq, A Report from Inside,* (2003), Granta Books, London, p. 180.
3. *Ibid.*
4. See, Angelo Colleoni (1984), *US Interventions: A Brief History,* Indian Revised edn., Sterling, New Delhi.

superpower ended all these restraints. The use of force in US foreign policy was legitimatised with or without the United Nations. The then US representative with UN, Madeleine Albright in early Clinton presidential administration, bluntly told the UN: "We will behave multilaterally when we can and unilaterally when we must."[5]

However, the last days of the stay of Bush I at the White House also were the last days when contempt for international law had not yet become totally open. A case in point was the First Gulf War when the 'regime change' and 'get Saddam' slogans were not attractive enough for US coalition partners. Besides, the former Soviet Union with its influential emissary to Iraq and an Arabicist, E. Primakov, though weak and well on way to final breakup, could not be totally ignored by President Bush I. This was the time for caution and prudent waiting for the demise of the USSR. In any case, in January-February 1991, US forces were not authorised by UN coalition to go beyond taking Kuwait back from Iraq. With the inauguration of Clinton presidency in January 1992 there were no hurdles to revive the interrupted US policy towards Iraq.

We have in an earlier chapter brought into focus how the US interests originated in the middle east during the closing stages of Second World War. Two compelling factors finally had drawn the attention of the Roosevelt administration: one was the huge reserves of oil in Arabia and the need for importing it for conserving US oil reserves, while the other was the issue of Jewish home in Palestine. As post-war years rolled on, and the Truman administration pursued its cold war with the Soviet Union and its allies intently, oil and a Jewish home in Palestine, now the State of Israel, gradually turned into decisive factors in US policy in the middle-east. Guided by these two main motivations, post-war US policy in the middle-east entered into treaty commitments with the State of Israel for its security and defence against the Arabs. It also moved to nurture client and suppliant Arab states in the region to ensure the continuity and growth of its stake in Arab oil,

5. As cited in Noam Chomsky, *op.cit.*, p. 73.

and to keep the erstwhile Soviet bloc engaged and away. The Suez crisis and Anglo-French-Israeli armed attack on Egypt gave the USA a portent opportunity to ease out the French stakes in the region and substantially reduce Britain's commitments in the region. In the mid-fifties, the USA played its cards comparatively successfully than other outside powers. A ring of client states, some formally declaring them as non-aligned, was nurtured so as to control their oil for the use of the USA and the west and to draw them into US military and defence orbit for the conduct of the cold war. The State of Israel was now being treated as a special category of dependable ally and partner, rather superstitiously, in view of susceptibilities of client Arab regimes, particularly the kingdom of Saudi Arabia.

Soon US policies in the region began to meet road blocks. For one thing, foreign policy of the Soviet Union had begun to win friends and sympathisers despite the traditional coolness of Arab regimes towards the causes it was espousing. For another, Arab nationalism had surged in open defiance of US-British control of Arab oil and it was challenging the essentials of US commitments to Israel. As always, Arab oil and the issue of a home for Jews in Palestine still shaped the contours of the region, though US-Soviet rivalry in the heydays of the cold war was an added input in them.

As a matter of fact, US foreign policy in the middle-east as elsewhere, was being influenced more and more by cold war basics under the control and guidance of the great cold war warrior, John Foster Dulles, the then US secretary of state. The Eisenhower era in US foreign policy, by all counts, was Dulles'.

The origin of US interests in Iraqi oil may be fruitfully traced in the Britain's stakes in it, even before the First World War. As mentioned earlier, oil was first found in commercial quantities in Masjid-i-Suleiman in Southern Iran near Iraqi Gulf coastline in 1908. The very next year Anglo-Persian Oil Company was formed and by 1914, the newly established Oil refinery at Abadan had begun exporting oil. A few days before the outbreak of the First World War in August 1914, the British government had acquired a 51 per cent holding of Anglo-

Persian Oil Company.[6]

At about the same time, rival international conglomerates, mainly German had begun making bids for oil concessions in Ottoman empire itself, particularly in Baghdad and Mosul *vilayats*. In 1902, a convention for building Baghdad—Berlin railway was signed between German banks and Ottoman authorities. This convention included mineral rights for German banks over land 20 kilometers each side of the track.[7] In 1912, 'African and Eastern concessions', guided by an Armenian—Ottoman and a successful business-engineer, S.C. Gulbenkian and with dominant British share-holdings managed to establish Turkish Petroleum Company (TPC) in 1912. Within months in 1913, TPC was merged with Anglo-Persian Oil Company. In August, 1914 the British government had acquired controlling share in Anglo-Persian Oil Company and as a result it also gained control of TPC, thereby access to known Iraqi oil rich areas. After the First World War, the British had established direct control on Iraq and its material resources under the mandate system of League of Nations. In March 1925 Britain managed the newly created Iraqi administration of its own choice in extracting almost exclusive rights for exploration of oil in Mosul region (a former Ottoman *vilayat*) through TPC, now linked with Anglo-Persian Oil Company. By 1927 oil was found in commercial quantities in Kirkuk area, north Iraq, near the Turkish border. The importance of Iraqi oil grew rapidly year by year. By 1934 Iraq was made dependent on oil revenues even for balancing its budgeted expenditure, small as it was.

Thus the State of Iraq by the time of its formal independence was tied down to its oil, controlled by Britain through (Iranian)-Turkish Petroleum Company (TPC).

At the time of its formation in 1912, the TPC was totally controlled by British interests comprising Royal Dutch Shell, the (British) National Bank of Turkey, Deutsche (German) Bank and C.S. Gulbenkian. After its merger with Anglo-Persian

---

6. Marion Farouk-Sluglett and Peter Sluglett (1987), *Iraq Since 1958, From Revolution to Dictatorship*, KPI Ltd., London, p. 8.
7. *Ibid.*

(Iranian) Oil Company in 1921, the controlling share of TPC, more than 67 per cent, came under the direct control of the British. By the end of twenties, TPC had stepped up its oil production and revenues, and as such, US oil companies had begun casting covetous glance at it. This was precisely the time when the Whitehall in London was finally preparing to prop up a subserviant Iraqi government for winding up its mandate in the face of growing anti-British feelings among the Iraqi population.

Two major US oil companies, Exxon and Mobil, had in July 1928 formed a 'Near East Development Company' for exploring oil in, what was called, Red line area, within the boundaries of former Ottoman empire, in fact, northern Iraq. Apparently with US pressure, these companies managed to sign a formal agreement for working with British oil companies in the region, Anglo-Persian (now BP), Royal Dutch Shell (in fact, a UK based company), French Totalfina Elf and the Armenian Istanbul entrepreneur and originator of TPC, Calouste S. Gulbenkian (who later formed his own Belgium based company, Partex, eventually branching out to Oman and UAE oil). In 1931 the name of Turkish Oil Company itself was changed into Iraq Petroleum Company (IPC) with its share distributed among the five as: 23.5 percent each to four companies—one British (Anglo-Persian, now BP), one British controlled (Royal Dutch Shell), one US, comprising Mobil and Exxon, one French (Totalfina Elf) and 5-6 percent shares allotted to C.S. Gulbenkian's business venture.[8] Now the IPC dominated Iraqi oil output for decades following.

The reconstitution of largely British controlled oil industry into IPC had nearly coincided with the end of British mandate and formal independence of Iraq in 1930. However, it was troublesome time for new Iraqi government of king Faisal, sandwitched between constant vigil of Britain and torn by domestic strife and growing anti-British sentiments. However, export of oil had by now replaced traditional export of Iraqi grain. Notwithstanding the foreign controlled Iraqi oil, the

8. For details see www.gulbenkian.

government had become dependent by 1934 on its oil revenues for balancing the budget. IPC was gaining importance year by year for its shareholders as well as for Iraqi government now totally controlled by Britain after Rashid Ali episode during the Second World War. As the table below shows, after the Second World War both oil production and its revenues had grown rapidly.

TABLE 1
Oil Production and Revenues 1946-1958

Year	*Million Tons*	*Revenue (ID Million)*
1946	4.6	2.3
1948	3.4	2.0
1950	6.5	5.3
1951	8.6	13.3
1953	28.0	49.9
1955	33.0	84.4
1958	35.8	79.9

Source : Y. Sayigh, *The Economies of the Arab World: Development since 1945*, p. 37. As cited in Sluglett (1987), *op.cit.*, p. 42.

In 1953, 49.3 per cent national income of Iraq was accounted by oil revenues. However, the Iraqi government had no role in production, price and export of Iraqi oil as IPC controlled all. Only a small fraction of growing oil revenues was given to Iraqi government. That too much was eaten up by growing corruption in the then Iraqi elite and grudgingly little was spent on long-term invisible projects like dam building and irrigation canals. Some major developments in the middle-east in early fifties, like the nationalisation of Iranian Oil in 1951 and Nasser's rise to power in Egypt in 1952 and later his successful defiance of Britain, France and Israel in 1956, had sparked off demonstrations and unrest in Iraq as well. The government of Nuri al-Said resorted to straightforward repression with UK-US patronage.

In July 1958, monarchy was overthrown but the new regime of Brigadier Qasim could hardly make a dent immediately to the growing money power and influence of IPC. It may be recalled that in February 1955 Iraq had joined the US sponsored military alliance, the Baghdad Pact, thereby formally ensuring US military foothold in the country for the present and future. In other words, Britain's hold over Iraq had been replaced not very long after the Second World War by the USA.

July 1958 coup d'etat was led by a group of nationalist 'free officers' headed by Karim Qasim, Salam Arif and Nagi Talib and not by any political party. However, split among them soon surfaced resulting in the removal of Arif as deputy prime minister and emergence of Qasim as 'sole leader' in October 1958. The politics of the leader of new regime[9] is not our concern here, and it need not detain us. Suffice to point out that Baath party, or any other political party, was not then in picture. The prime motivating force at the beginning was nationalism as articulated by elite officers of British trained Iraqi army. It had in view also a control on the burst of conspicuous consumption by Iraqi establishment due to sudden rise in oil revenues since early fifties.

However, decision on pressing issues, inherited from the ancient regime had to be taken immediately for legitimising its overthrow by force. Monarchy was abolished, as the country withdrew from the Baghdad Pact and it declared non-alignment in foreign policy. It also professed, like Nasser, full commitment to Arab solidarity and support for Arab cause in Palestine. Very soon it broke the Iraqi version of Berlin war and established diplomatic relations with the former Soviet Union, other Socialist countries and China. All these took place by the end of fifties. Qasim's Iraq thus showed that the new government no longer intended to become subservient to the policies of the USA, Britain and the West. These moves clearly infuriated the west, the USA in particular.

Eisenhower doctrine was proclaimed on March 9, 1957. This authorised the US president to use force at his discretion against any middle-east country which was not tuned to US foreign policy goals. US military intrusion in Lebanon was particularly unwelcome in July 1958 to the new Iraqi regime because the Lebanese towns of Sidon and Tripoli carried Iraqi

9. For useful insight, see Ch. 2 in Sluglett (1987), *op. cit.*

oil pipeline from its oil refineries nearby. These were of course early days, much more was to come later.

In all probability, Washington was not unaware of growing instability of Nuri al-Said government in Iraq. By all counts, it had made initial preparations for what British called "filling the vacuum in east of Suez" after its debacle over Suez Canal. Pentagon had already made a beginning as early as 1949 by establishing naval base facilities in Bahrain in Indian ocean on a lease from Britain. Later after the Suez crisis, it had also built military staging facility at Oman's Masira island. Let us also recall that by the time Karim Qasim had successfully staged his coup, Baghdad was already a full-fledged member of Baghdad Pact for about three years and its military co-operation and coordination with fellow members of the alliance had advanced with contingents of British army stationed near Baghdad and its environments.

Hence, US response to Qasim coup was immediate and swift. On the very next day of the coup, July 15, 1958, the USA landed its marines on the beaches south of Lebanon's capital, Beirut, in close proximity of Iraq. The alleged pretext was to protect the pro-US Lebanese president, Camille Chamoun. Two other important developments of the time had directly impacted on US response. The one was rising tide of nationalism under Gamal Abdul Nasser's leadership sweeping through the Arab lands causing sleepless nights to the leaders of US Arab satellites.

The other was concessionary rights for exploration to Iraqi Petroleum Company (IPC). Most Iraqi nationalists did understand that Iraqi oil was the main issue of explosive nature. Qasim regime moved in pursuing its nationalist agenda on oil. The Iraqi government was interested in exporting more oil under its own control and this it could do from huge oil reserves in and around Mosul. The Iraqi government therefore withdrew under law 80 in 1961, oil concession in 160,000 sq. miles of southern Iraq territory originally given to IPC. Meanwhile, in 1964 Iraqi National Oil Company (INOC) was formed to exploit these lands including oil rich Rumalia. But it had hardly the money or infrastructure. The IPC challenged the law 80, and some compromise was reached. After long drawn-out meetings, INOC was given wide power to develop Rumalia oil field near Basra. The IPC still had not reconciled to new situation and continued to apply pressure; so much so that it cut the output of Kirkuk oilfields by half in March 1972.

The IPC was warned but they did not listen. Finally, the government nationalised the IPC in June 1972. Iraq became the first Arab country to take over western oil companies and to nationalise oil industry.

As a consequence of nationalisation of IPC, five major foreign oil cartels lost out; two US based, two US-UK based, one primarily based in France, a poor third. Major shareholders in the IPC at the time of nationalization were: Shell, BP, ESSO (later Exxon), Mobil and CFP, the French national company. Soon after nationalization, Iraq turned to Russian (Soviet Union) for funds and partnership. The former Soviet government was given exclusive right of exploration in Rumalia and Basra, while France was not far behind. The western companies were keen to regain control over oil. Besides, they were unhappy that their rivals, Russians, French, even Chinese had stepped in and they might gain global long-term advantage in oil business at their cost.[10]

Five oil companies, two US based, two UK based and one French-Italian have traditionally dominated the world oil industry. The US based Exxon Mobil ranks today first and the biggest company. The USA thus ranks first in corporate oil sector, with UK second and France trailing a distant third.[11]

As mentioned earlier, US foreign policy and oil have always been interlinked. Free access to world oil resources have been a major goal post of US foreign policy of long standing. Iraq's oil wealth has become everybody's business, above all, the USA. As *Investor's and Business Daily* noted on September 20, 2002; If the US were to occupy Iraq it would not only "gain a central staging base for future (military) operations", but it would take control of 11 percent of world oil reserves too ...and

10. Anthony Arnove, ed. (2002), *op.cit.*, pp. 94-95.
11. In order of size, these five oil companies are: Exxon Mobil, Royal Dutch-Shell, British Petroleum (BP)-Amoco, Chevron-Texaco and Totalfina Elf., *Ibid.*, p. 99.

it could also be a leverage against oil-dependant Arab nations."[12]

Yet another prime motivation of US involvement in the middle-east had originated with the issue of a Jewish home in Palestine, put on the international agenda by Britain through its historic Belfour Declaration of 1917. We have earlier mentioned how US President Woodrow Wilson got interested in the issue of Jewish settlement in Palestine. During the closing stages of World War II, when on 14 February, 1945 President Roosevelt met Saudi king, Abdul Aziz Ibn Saud on board the US warship *Quincy* in Great Bitter lake, he sought Ibn Saud's help in the problem of Palestine. But he also listened his guest and formally promised to the king consultation and protection to the Arabs over the Palestine question.[13] But after his sudden death, the interim president Harry Truman disregarded the promises of Roosevelt. He had explained to his advisers six months later with coming presidential election in mind:

> "I am sorry gentleman but I have to answer to hundreds of thousands who are anxious for the success of Zionism; I do not have hundreds of thousands of Arabs among my constituents."[14]

The state of Israel was thus formed with active US support and encouragement in 1948 and close US-Israel multifaced relations followed. The US involvement in the middle-east was now a fact of international life, while oil and Israel emerged as its essentials, certainly from the very end of the Second World War. This just about preceded the formal beginning of the cold war as both the USA and the USSR had then cooperated in getting the UN approval for the division of Palestine in 1947, which had paved the way for the emergence of independent State of Israel in 1948. The cold war, however, soon became one of its main sources of survival and development. Many conservative Arab regimes, like in Saudi Arabia, wrongly thought that keeping the USA on their side during the cold war and later, might ensure their security and also give them

12. *Ibid.*, p. 96.
13. Robert Lacey (1982), *op. cit.*, pp. 270-74, p. 274.
14. *Ibid.*, p. 275.

more space for dealing with Israel and gaining real control of their oil. The USA did not, however, reward them and the post-cold war international environment proved non-conducive to their aspirations.

Unfortunately, successive post-Second World War US administrations sought to find favourable environment for their policies in the middle-east by doubtful means—creating clients and strengthening despots, in the Arab world, openly setting aside the fundamental ideas of US Constitution and its practice. The first Gulf War 1991 had, however, showed the way for US hegemony—the use of brute force. Those who shown doubts or dared to confront US policies in the middle east were marked as foes and adversaries. This panaroma began to unfold ever since the rise of Nasser in February 1952 in Egypt. Iraq and its people became current US targets. We shall quickly look in the following pages this sad saga of US foreign policy in contemporary middle-east.

Iraqi Internal Politics/USA

It is not our case that post-Second World War US policy worked in a straightline consistently with well-defined objectives and set goal-posts. It had its ups and downs, successes and failures, but its primary motivations continued to be operative. The question, however, arises: why Iraq and its leadership, particularly under Saddam Husain had angered successive US administrations beyond their own traditional constraints ever since July 1958. So much so that President Bush II administration had developed a fixation about Saddam Husain and Iraq. In seeking to understand this phenomenon, we may fruitfully look at domestic development in Iraq after the assassination of Iraqi president Karim Qasim in February 1963.

These domestic developments in Iraq were dirty and mirky, certainly a nightmare for outside observers. However, a few of its relevant features could be sorted out. First, July 1958 coup d'etat was a military take-over led by 19th and 20th Infantry Brigades of British trained Iraqi army; brutal force was widely employed against the leaders and supporters and institutions, real or imaginary, of the ancient regime, such as monarchy and two chambers of rump parliament. Hence the role of army turned more crucial than ever before perhaps not intended by its British patrons.

During the Qasim years, 1958-1963, political parties, including Baath party and Iraqi Communist Party (ICP) did take to public demonstrations and political posturings, though they had no role in July 1958 events. Over the years both the Baath party and ICP gained ascendancy generating bitter rivalry and animosity between them. The coup against Qasim in February 1963 was organised and executed by Baath party with some nationalist elements through its irregular paramilitary force, the National Guard, whose number was estimated to have risen from 5000 to 34000 between February and August 1963. The coup was also mainly directed at eliminating ICP which had by then became probably the strongest and most popular communist party in the middle east. In eliminating the ICP and their supporters between February and November 1963, Iraq saw "some of the most terrible scenes of violence hitherto experienced in the post-war Middle East."[15]

It was also during these months of 1963, that National Guard ran the government with an iron hand, whose commanders like notorious Mundhir al-Wandhwai, took orders directly from the Secretary-General of Baath party who in turn was a notorious gang leader himself.[16]

This situation continued until yet another coup de'tat in November 1963, still controlled by Baath party, now led by Salam Arif with the active support of the army. Arif's regime lasted till April 1966 but its most important contribution was the creation of an elite corps, the 'Republican Guards', initially manned by the men from 20th Infantry Brigade, one of the main armed units of July revolution. It also went down well in the history of contemporary Iraq by a summary dismantling of National Guard and the dismissal of its notorious commander, Wandhwai.[17]

15. Sluglett (1987), *op.cit.*, p. 85.
16. *Ibid.*, p. 87.
17. *Ibid.*, pp. 93-94.

After 1963, the influence of Baath party declined mainly because of its propensity to violence, while conservative nationalists, not necessarily Nasserites, gained ascendancy. The government was however, torn between factions and became inactive. The crisis came with Iraq's failure in participating even as a token in 1967 Arab-Israeli war, inspite of Iraq's loud claim of being a front-line state against Israel. Finally, after accidental death of Salam Arif as president of Iraqi Republic in April 1966, Baath party took power in a coup d'etat on 17 July 1968. It founded a seven-man Revolutionary Command Council (RCC) consisting entirely of officers.[18] In a subsequent coup a few weeks after, Baath party succeeded in taking a firm control of RCC. The party was now in power and the rise of Saddam Husain came simultaneously.

From 1968 to 1969, Saddam was the real power behind al-Bakr, then president. In 1969 Saddam became vice-president emerging as the real power-centre of the regime. After the resignation of ailing and ageing al-Bakr on July 16, 1979, the RCC elected Saddam Husain as President of the Iraqi Republic. Saddam remained in control until US forces overthrew his government in April 2003. The Bush II doctrine of regime change by the brutal use of force as per its convenience was finally put into practice over a small nation, defeated and exhausted even before.

Baath Party

At this stage, it is worthwhile to look at the origin and development of Baath party in Iraq. Baath party was founded in Damascus in 1944 by three French-educated Syrian intellectuals led by Michel Aflaq, a Greek orthdox Christian. At that time Syria was still under French mandate and it was really intended as a movement against French rule. The party soon expanded rapidly. By 1954, sixteen Baathists were elected to Syrian parliament and it had spread to neighbouring regions with its distinct pan-Arab ideology.

The ideas of Baath party reached Iraq by 1949.[19] In 1951,

18. For details of RCC, see *Ibid.*, p. 114.
19. For well sourced details of early history of Baath Party, see, Sluglett (1987), *op.cit.*, pp. 87-93.

there developed a small party organisation with about fifty members led by a shia engineer from Nasiriya, Faud al-Rikabi. By 1955, its membership had grown to 289, most of them shias and friends and relatives of Rikabi. In 1957, Rikabi made Baath party join opposition National Front alongwith communists and others. The party had to work underground as Nuri al-Said government had declared opposition parties illegal. It had supported the July 1958 take-over and its aftermath. At that time, it was reported to have, according to Rikabi himself, "300 active members, 1200 organised helpers (Ansars), 2000 organised supporters and 10,000 unorganised supporters."[20]

However, the Iraqi Baath party had no role in July 1958 events. But within few months it joined hands with nationalists in opposing Qasim, communists and their supporters on the programme of Arab unity on the model of merger of Syria and Egypt. In November 1959, the party took its first major step by attempting an unsuccessful attempt to assassinate Qasim; Saddam Husain, who had joined Baath party in 1957 at the age of twenty was the member of this murder squad. He was wounded in the attempt and took refuge in Syria and then Egypt until 1963. By February 1963, Baathist army officers had begun staging coup d'etats against established Iraqi regime. Saddam Husain remained active on his return from exile in 1963, and as described earlier, emerged as its leader by 1969.

Baath party was in disarry by the end of 1959 mainly as a consequence of its failed attempt on the life of Qasim. al-Rikabi had founded a rival body in 1961. By 1966 the Syrian Baath party had also split. It had snapped its links with Iraqi Baath party, despite the presence in Baghdad of Michel Aflaq, the original founder of Baath party.

The programme of the party was at no time consistent or systematic, and it was changed or adjusted from time to time. Broadly speaking, it had two main proclaimed objectives, Arab socialism and Arab unity, while a common framework was Arab nationalism vis-a-vis outside powers. Such a programme was essentially inspired by Nasserites of the Arab world,

---

20. *Ibid.*, p. 90.

though it was communicated in extremely wide and vague terms, thereby more suitable for declamatory speeches and communiques. However, the basic orientation of Iraqi Baath party was to Arab socialism, like that of Nasserites, anti-communism and anti-Marxism. No wonder that the practical experience of merger of Egypt and Syria in 1958 turned out a failure within a few years in 1961.

Iraqi Baathists stoutly opposed moves for Iraq's merger with Egypt or any other state. On the other hand, the idea of Arab socialism was made sufficiently flexible by them with the sole exception of consistency in their suppression and brutality against Iraqi communists. However, it remained anti-imperialist. For example, article 26 of the constitution of Baath party (both in Syria and Iraq) stressed: "The party of Arab Baath is a socialist party. It believes that the economic wealth of fatherland belongs to the nation".[21]

Majid Khadduri, a noted Iraqi scholar and an ardent supporter of Iraqi Baathists in early Saddam years, had suggested that the Iraqi Baath party was a highly organised and structured party, comparable in many ways to a communist party.[22] This suggestion is obviously subjective and an exaggeration. Yet Iraqi Baath party had certainly been a unique phenomenon in the middle-east with a possible exception of Syria. It always had an organization and a programme, but personal relationships and common sectarian and geographical origins, and not ideological commitments, had always been decisive.

More importantly, the party was loosely interconnected conspirational group, like-minded friends and relatives wanting to capture power and hold to it with the support of elite military men loyal to the Baathist regime, later to be known as Presidential Guards. Seizing of power and holding to it by military support and through the use of violence and suppression, and not through ballot boxes, was the main

21. Cited in *Ibid.*, p. 89.
22. Majid Khadduri (1987), *Socialist Iraq: A Study in Iraqi Politics Since 1968*, Middle East Institute, Washington, pp. 36-41.

modus operandi of Iraqi Baath party. In this very sense, the Iraqi party probably was always different than its parent organization in Syria.

Yet the activities of Baath party in post-July 1958 Iraq, were hardly countered seriously in the country, although these were proscribed between 1963 and 1968. Half-hearted attempts were made and Saddam Husain himself claimed to have been arrested and imprisoned in 1964.

However, anti-imperialist character of Baath regime was not in serious doubt, notwithstanding the quick waverings, rash actions and authoritarian rule of Saddam Husain, 'the sole leader' of the country, nay of the Iraqi people, as he was never tired of claiming. Hence, the USA, the hyperpower of post-cold war years, had some extra special reasons for targeting Iraq and 'the villain of Baghdad', Saddam Husain.

5

USA AND SADDAM

President George W. Bush (Bush II) and his conservative advisers and think-tanks have currently found a new version of 'the thief of Baghdad', a popular and likeable character of medieval Arab classical tales, *Arabian Nights*—"the villain of Baghdad". We are told, "the villain of Baghdad" is despicable and brutal, indeed a scourge for each and every noble features of our contemporary civilization; above all, he is alive, reported to be still fighting the unprecedented might of US missiles and marines even in defeat and deprivation. Who made this man, now about 66 years old, into a villain? Not certainly God did it, nor he did it only on his own. He got help, real help, from none other than from the leadership of the USA and its main ally, the UK.

When the British created and nurtured Iraqi administration was overthrown in July 1958, Saddam Husain was hardly twentyone years old student of Baghdad. He had about less than a year earlier in 1957 joined a small group of friends and relatives, calling themselves Baath party on the model of its parent body in neighbouring Syria. Even this small group had to sit together under cover because of fear and suppression of Nuri al-Said government. In any case, Saddam Husain and his Baath party had absolutely nothing to do with the nationalist minded group of army officers, led by Qasim and Arif. Not that Saddam Husain was totally apolitical, unaware of the issues of the day. His guardian maternal uncle, a retired army officer, had very often talked of his anguish on Britain's domination over Iraq in his house in a village near Tikrit, then a small town on the Tigris river, north of Baghdad. This indeed was a political education in the classical traditions of 5000 years old history of the region. In 1954 he had moved to his uncles' house in Baghdad.

The July 1958 events had provided an opportunity for political parties and groups, including the Baathists, to break cover and function openly. The Iraqi Communist Party (ICP), founded in secrecy in 1934, made most of the opportunity and rapidly gained mass support within a year. The Baathists also utilised the opportunity by focusing attention on Pan-Arabism a'la Nasser. But relations between Nasser and Qasim had by the end of 1958 soured. After the removal of the co-leader of July 1958 coup, Salem Arif, in November 1958, Qasim had begun leaning more and more on ICP. The political environment in Baghdad by summer of 1959, had thus turned non-conducive to small group of Baathist and Nasserite nationalists. By the close of 1958, Nasser had himself begun to debunk all Arab communists publicly in his characteristic style. Iraqi communists also came up for criticism all over the Arab world for pressurising the Qasim regime. Such acts of foreign policy of the Qasim regime, as withdrawal of Iraq from the Baghdad Pact and establishment of diplomatic relations with the then Communist bloc—were now ignored by Iraqi Nasserite nationalists. With its origin and development as a small conspiratorial group, the Baathists took the lead in covert planning against the Qasim government. They staged failed revolt in Mosul in March 1959, then an attempt at the assassination of Qasim himself in broad daylight in the main street of Baghdad on 7 October, 1959. The three-man murder squad included Saddam Husain. Karim Qasim was unhurt but Saddam got injured seriously and managed to escape to exile in Syria and then in Egypt until 1963. The fact that al-Rikabi, the founder of Iraqi Baath party, and then secretary-general was involved in the plot, did indicate that by mid-1959 Saddam had already risen fairly high in echelons of the party, however small it might well be.[1]

1. For details, see Sluglett. (1987), *op.cit.*, p. 73.

What he did during his exile in Cairo, no account was available. However, it is now known that he studied law in Cairo University and watched closely Nasser and his supporters in action. On returning to Baghdad he married his uncle's daughter and resumed his activities. This might well be in early 1963 as he was reported to have been actively involved in unprecedented widespread violence of February-November 1963, mainly directed against communists and their supporters.

This unprecedented massacre of communists during February-November 1963, following the overthrow of Qasim, was certainly carefully planned and well executed. It had taken place after the Cuban missile crisis and against the backdrop of growing Soviet involvement in Egypt, rising surge of Arab nationalism, above all, of militarization, of US role in the middle-east even near the Iraqi borderlands.

Here it may be recalled, that marines from US sixth fleet, then positioned in the Gulf, had landed on the beaches of Lebanon, a near neighbour, on July 15, 1958 within twentyfour hours of July 1958 events in Iraq on the publicised plea of saving Lebanon from the raging civil war. Lebanon's civil war lasted for years, and consequently, US military presence continued in the country. This was a vantage position to watch the events in Baghdad and to restrain Baghdad from its impending withdrawal from the Baghdad Pact and developing ties with the former Soviet bloc. It was also not coincidental that important oil pipe terminals of Iraq Petroleum Company (IPC) at Sidon and Tripoli, both in Lebanon, were within an easy range of the sixth fleet and its marines.

Given the fact that US was closely monitoring events in Iraq, particularly after its exit from the Baghdad Pact, in September 1958, it was perhaps logical for USA to gain a foothold in Iraqi politics and not to rely solely on US oil company share-holders in IPC and rich Iraqi non-residents. Baath party and its young leaders, like Saddam, who had begun opposing the Qasim regime almost from its day one, were now important targets. It is now confirmed that the CIA was in close touch with some prominent young Baathist leaders including Saddam Husain from 1959 onwards. In 1963 it had most probably a crucial role in overthrowing Qasim and in brutual suppression of communists through the Baathists including Saddam Husain.[2]

During 1959-1963, both the US government and Iraqi nationalists and Baathists, including Saddam Husain, had obviously a common vested interest in regime-change as well as in suppressing the communists and their sympathisers who were gaining more and more mass support under a tolerant Qasim regime.

The regime that took to power in February 1963 was a coalition of nationalists and Baathists. Both jockeyed for absolute power with prominent and powerful members of the new apparatus who had become more and more ruthless gangleaders than mere supporters of the new regime. Soon they fell out by November 1963, the Baathists were themselves divided on the questions of Arab unity and Arab socialism. As a matter of fact, February-November 1963 was a period of anarchy, confusion and beastly violence in Iraq. It was no wonder that friends and foes of Iraq, including perhaps the CIA, did not quite understand which way Iraq was heading. However, by December 1963 Baath party was banned and its leading members like Saddam imprisoned. But this ban was never seriously pursued by the new regime of Abd al-Salam Arif. Saddam slipped out of prison to exile once again, came back to Baghdad within months and as earlier, he resumed his activities.

All this did leave a scar on Iraqi society, and consequently, to a paralysis of Arif's regime. The sudden death of Salam Arif in an air crash in April 1966 compounded the confusion. Such a situation in Iraq suited all, the USA, Israel and the West and its Arab regional antagonists. A striking example here was the vaccilation of the successor regime, headed by Arif's brother, Abdul Rahman in coming to Egypt's help in six-day Arab-Israel war of June 1967, despite its trumpeted commitments against Israel. Protests and demonstrations,

2. Authoritative sources in confirmation are cited in *Ibid.*, pp. 85-86.

mostly led by Baathists, turned into usual features of life in Baghdad. Finally, on 17 July 1968, Baath party succeeded in staging another coup and captured power. After yet another coup on 30 July, 1968 the Revolutionary Command Council (RCC) was reconstituted with Saddam formally becoming vice-president of the Republic. Thus began the rise of Saddam as a power centre behind President al-Bakr, an ageing 56 year old former major-general of presidential guard.

In the meantime, Saddam Husain and his associates in the party appeared to have learnt their lessons from the debacles of September 1959 and November 1963. They had built up the party, infiltrated in the army command and in the national guards and sought to reorganise the economy. Indeed the entire country was assiduously built-up under the leadership of Saddam Husain after 1968. It was also precisely during this period that he developed the reputation of a ruthless tough and highly motivated strongman of the party and government.

With al-Bakr's cooperation, he eased out his opposition, ongoing or potential, in the RCC. The Islamic revolution in Iran in January 1979 provided him yet another opportunity which he seized characteristically. On July 16, 1979, he himself became President of the Republic as well as the RCC after al-Bakr had resigned. From that time onward, Saddam was the sole leader, the only power-centre in Iraq.

The events described above were crucial for Iraq and defined the contours of international politics in the region, and later in the world. It should be a naivety even to suggest that its main antagonists, the USA and its regional satellite states, were simply watching them with awe and wonder. So what were they doing?

Without repeating ourselves, let us recall that the USA and the west were thoroughly alarmed by July 14, 1958 coup de'tat in Iraq. Show of force and the threat to use it, overt diplomacy and covert intelligence, all were unleashed immediately on a small and still poor nation, like Iraq, then led by Abdul Karim Qasim. Right from September 1959, Saddam Husain had emerged as a top favourite of CIA, and the then Iraqi president was the main target. As politics and power struggle among various factions and groups in Iraq got mirkier and nastier, the secret services of Saudis, Iranians, Jordanians, Israelies joined CIA and MI 6 in this toppling game. Finally, with such help readily available, Qasim was overthrown and killed. Above all, in the bargain, Iraqi communists were massacred and brutually eliminated. This was February-November 1963 in the history of modern Iraq with Baath party in power and Saddam Husain as one of its zealous young emerging leader.

Despite the counter-coup of November 1963, and consequent outlawing of Baath party and arrest of Saddam Husain, it hardly ever diluted its activities. The USA during 1963-68 had other things to worry about in the region and got diverted. It showed more interest in keeping the Shah of Iran in power, helping and abetting Israel, and taming the Libiyan leader Gaddafi. Yet the instability and in-fighting of Iraqi regime were certainly encouraged and abetted from outside, mainly the USA and Britain.

The Baathists came to power again as a result of two coup de'tats in quick succession on July 17 and July 30, 1968. As mentioned earlier, Saddam was already in command, while the Iraqi army and its Presidential Guard were his main tools. In this confusing and murky world of Iraqi politics during 1963-1968, it was not difficult to see how hostile foreign powers, particularly the USA and Israel, could not have been mute spectators. We still do not have concrete evidence, but our opinion here is surely not imaginary and motivated.

On the other hand, developments in Iraq since July 1968 under Baathist regime do also point to sudden snapping of links between CIA and other friendly secret services and Baath party leaders, including Saddam. This was the story until the Islamic revolution in Iran and Saddam becoming President of Iraq in 1979.

Let us now turn back to events unfolding since July 1968.

By July 30, 1968, Baath party was in total control of Revolutionary Command Council (RCC) with Saddam as its vice-president. Soon after, the Baath party was formally separated from its parent Syrian body, while Michel Aflaq, one of its three founders was made the secretary-general of the Baghdad based party. Saddam Husain was still assistant secretary-general of the party, but the party now under his control, had begun to transform itself into an instrument of power, coercion and suppression. Meanwhile, Iraq's relations with the USA were steadily going downhill in the wake of open military and diplomatic support to Israel in its six-day war with Arabs in June 1967. The then Iraqi non-Baathist president of Iraq had broken off diplomatic relations with the USA in August 1967 in protest. Be it noted that at that time Saddam and Baath party were still making preparations for their coup de'tat. It was obvious that the streets of Baghdad had turned against the USA and its overt support to Israel, in particular. Anti-US sentiments were growing day-by-day. The new dispensation under Saddam saw no reason to restrain it. More so, after the 1968 US presidential election had focused on the issue of arming Israel against its Arab neighbours in a bid of winning Jewish votes for rival candidates.

On the other hand, the new regime in Iraq took a series of steps rapidly that had still more infuriated the Nixon and Ford administrations. The one, it sought to control its own oil wealth, after tortuous negotiations with Iraq Petroleum Company (IPC) that essentially failed, IPC was nationalised without compensation and taken over by the state owned Iraq National Oil Company (INOC) in June 1972. Esso (later Exxon) and Mobil—US companies, Shell, BP—UK companies who had long held a three quarter share in IPC, and the French national company, CFP—all, lost their commanding position and entire money. The other, the Saddam government had really turned in 1968 to the former Soviet Union for help and assistance in extracting oil from oil rich Rumelia in oil technology and credit, thus Soviet (Russian) role in Iraq's national economy and political life grew year by year. Soon, French broke ranks and also joined hands, with INOC. But the US and UK companies were kept aside. Yet production and export earning of Iraqi oil grew by leaps and bounds, as for instance, from 1.3 million barrel per day (b/d) in 1965 to 3.4 million per day (b/d) in 1979.[3] Although the rate of growth dipped during Iraq-Iran

3. *Exxon Background Series*, "Middle East Oil and Gas", December 1984.

war, 1980-88, it picked up quickly after its end, bayoneted by the rise in global petrol prices.

Consequent upon nationalization of IPC and astounding rapid rise in reserves of petro-dollars the quality of life for the Iraqi people had vastly improved. Even the small landholders of rural segment, perhaps the in the region, turned better. The living standard of Iraqi's in the eighties was growing, corruption in top Iraqi establishments, notwithstanding.

It also led to modernization of fire power of Iraqi army with credit assistance for arms purchases from the former Soviet Union and France. The west noted these developments with anxiety; an unprovoked Israeli air-strike at Iraq's nuclear installations in July 1987 was symptomatic in itself. The Saddam regime became more confident of its acceptance, nay popularity, among the proverbial man/woman in the streets and by-lanes of Iraq. A modern prosperous, and above all, secular Iraq, a rare exception in the Arab world, had grown up by the beginning of 90s.

Since its very birth, Iraq was dominated by outsiders and exploited by UK and US oil corporations. Now it could not go back in history. The despotic and coercive instruments of indigenous rule were no issues of crucial nature for this new Iraq.

Looking back with the benefit of hindsight, it should be considered perhaps logical that the US policy-makers would extract the benefits of their past contacts with Saddam after he had grabbed power in July 1968. Surely, they were angered by snapping of diplomatic relations with the USA by the previous Iraqi government. Later, the loss of hold of US-UK oil cartels on Iraqi oil and growing proximity of Saddam with Nasser and the then Soviet leaders were added worries for the USA, then fully engaged in Vietnam war. However, it moved in reinforcing US air bases around *Aramco* oil installations in Dhahran, Saudi Arabia which was operational since January 1957.

Suddenly on 28 September, 1970, President Nasser of Egypt died of a heart attack. This death had totally changed the Arab scenario rapidly and a vacuum in Arab leadership was felt alround. The new Egyptian president, Anwar Sadat made a bid to step in Arab leadership vacuum, but the military stalemate of 1973 Arab-Israeli war could not wash away the shame of Arab defeat in the six-day war of 1967. US President Nixon had ordered massive airlifting of US arms and equipments openly and without any hesitation to Israel during 1973 war, much against the pleas of its chief Arab ally and cheap oil-supplier, Saudi Arabia.

This was precisely the kind of environment that Saddam really wanted for making a bid for the leadership of the Arab world in his chosen Nasserite fashion. He moved fast and effectively, as described earlier. Two later developments proved still more conducive for Saddam, the Camp David Egypt-Israel accord of winter 1978-79 and consequent formalization of Arab disunity, on the one hand, and the fall of Shah of Iran and Islamic revolution in Iran a year later, in January-February 1979, on the other. Saddam made a direct bid for Arab summit in Baghdad in November 1978 against the impending Camp David accord. This, however, proved abortive mainly because of firm opposition from Saudi Arabia.[4] On the other end, the Islamic revolution was still surging ahead aspiring to engulf Iraq as well, despite US machinations against it.

Saddam's personal friend and the then Arabist ambassador of the former USSR, Eugine Primakov, had no doubt begun hinting to Saddam at inner decay of his country. Further help and assistance from it correctly appeared to him in mid-eighties a distant possibility.

Saddam's Iraq felt threatened. It gave up any pretension of Arab leadership, a position hotly contested by Saudi Arabia as well with US blessings. Like other contemporary leaders of the Arab world, this time around Saddam himself sought friendship with a rich and powerful former patron, the USA. He, however, miscalculated by precipitating a war against neighbouring Iran in March 1980. This war turned out as a purposeless war of heavy loss of men and materials for both Iran and Iraq. Meanwhile, Saddam restored diplomatic relations with the USA in November 1984, although trade and

4. For details, see Robert Lacey (1982), pp. 455-58.

diplomatic contacts during UN meetings had begun picking up as early as 1974.[5] Obviously, both the USA and Iraq had decided to forget the past in the face of a common enemy, Iran.

Such a turnabout in US-Iraq relations was obviously not the handiwork of Saddam alone; the US administration was no less involved. As a matter of fact, the Reagan and Bush I administrations had turned Saddam into their "favourite guy" ever since the beginning of 1980s.[6] The USA soon emerged "as a primary diplomatic supporter, a provider of military intelligence and very crucially a provider of weapons of mass destruction, including biological chemical materials".[7] Such all-inclusive US support enabled Iraq to conduct war against Iran for eight long years and also to use chemical weapons against its own Kurdish citizens in Halabja in northern Iraq in 1988 as well as against the Iranian troops.[8] So much so that Reagan and Bush I administrations had increased subsidized food aid to Iraq, as Iraq, traditionally self-sufficient in food, had faced shortages in late eighties as a consequence of devastation of fertile agricultural lands in the north by gassing of Kurds.[9]

Thus the aggression against Iran and inhuman devastation of Kurds throughout the eighties drew support and sustenance from the USA. Why?

Firstly, in Iraq-Iran war, the USA chose to extend support to a side which in its views was weaker and lesser evil, Iraq. It sought to balance the imbalance between the two so that they might continue fighting until they exhaust to mutual destruction, hence a cake-walk for the USA in the region. Later, this policy was termed as a policy of dual containment. In the eighties, Iran was considered a bigger challenge. Islamic Iran, after all, had cost President Jimmy Carter his re-election in 1980. As among other important factors, he had failed to free

---

5. See, Sluglett, (1987), *op.cit.*, pp. 282-83, p. 310.
6. Anthony Arnove, ed., (2002), *op.cit.*, p. 57.
7. *Ibid.*, pp. 57-58.
8. *Ibid.*
9. Noam Chomesky (2003), p. 66.

US hostages in Tehran. *Secondly,* a logical explanation appeared to have yet another important dimension. This had far more to do with international situation than with regional situation alone. At the beginning of eighties, the age-old direct mechanism of concession and control of Iraqi and Iranian oil was a walk back in time; so much so that Saudi Araba's popular US oriented oil minister, Ahmad Zaki Yamani, had begun in 1981 demanding a total control of shares from US oil giant, *Aramco.* Besides, Gaddafi, of oil rich Libya, had launched a concerted campaign against US stooges in the region—Sadat and the Saudi king. Moreover, tiny independent-client states brimming with oil, like UAE, Oman, Qatar, were put in place by the British. On top of it all, there were recurring crises in another super-power, the then USSR, that could have led to its instability, consequently in global power-structure.

In July 1981, in the above scenario, the only super-power gaining in strength under Reagan and later Bush I administration, felt more responsible than ever before to assert its traditional linkage with cheap and easily available Arab oil. Although the USA was not totally dependent on Arab oil, its close allies, Japan, Germany, UK and other West Europeans were dependent on it for their spiral of prosperity and power. So the issue, then before the USA, was not that the Arabs would take away their oil but how to keep the supply line open, stable and cheap for the US and its allies; also, how to block others like the former Soviet Union, France and then China in Arab oil market. The USA, a post-Second World War traditional dominant force in the middle-east and the world was well on the way of becoming, what the French now call a "hyperpower". Above all, it must be in control of access to the middle-east oil for "security and stability" of its own and its allies.

With such no-hold barred US support, Saddam considered himself victorious in 1988, at the end of a long drawn-out brutal war, notwithstanding 240,000 Iraqi deaths and about 112 billion US dollar expenditure and massive loans of 83 billion dollar for buying arms and equipments (8 billion US dollars from the Soviet Union, 25-35 billion US dollars from the west and Japan, and 50-55 billion US dollars from Saudi Arabia, Kuwait and other Gulf emirates).[10] He plunged his administration in reconstruction of war ravaged country employing extensively cheap foreign workers, though he felt hampered by stringent loan offers from fellow Arab countries, particularly Kuwait. It was at this juncture that the USA once again took a hand. Its overactive ambassador in Baghdad, Avril Glaspie, indeed encouraged Saddam to seek the help of his brother Arab states like rich Kuwait for reconstruction. On the other end, the USA was reported to have advised the Kuwait leadership not to get pressurised by Iraqi's demands. In any case, the USA considered Iraq-Kuwait relations bilateral that could be dealt with the assistance of collective Arab efforts. The USA did not want to interfere either way for Iraq or for Kuwait—they were told.[11] The talks with Kuwait at Jeddah and elsewhere had failed, perhaps because the USA just watched, nay, encouraged both sides to be firm and steadfast against each other.

Saddam apparently saw through the US game after his ego-trip, in his views, successful, in launching a war with Iran. If he had decided to force the hands of the USA vis-a-vis Kuwait, like in Iraq-Iran war, he had miscalculated, rather foolishly.

At early dawn of August 2, 1990, Iraq's elite six Republican Guard divisions had moved seventyfive miles inside Kuwait from southern Iraqi desert, and occupied Kuwait city within four hours. The first Gulf war had begun. A regional issue soon turned into a global issue of all UN concern. God has blessed America once again!

There was never any love lost between Kuwait and Iraq and in the late eighties Iraq might have genuine grievances against Kuwait. But its invasion was yet another big, by then familiar, mistake of Saddam. The fact that the USA, it is now known, might well have misguided him deliberately could

10. Dilip Hiro (2003), *op.cit.*, p. 32. Iran's loss was close, but less with no foreign loans.
11. Frequent long meetings of US ambassador with Saddam Husain during late 1980s, reportedly on the issue of Iraq's demands for loans from Kuwait, were amply covered in US media. See Dilip Hiro (2003), *op.cit.*, p. 34.

never absolve him of his stupid miscalculations for a number of obvious reasons.

First of all, the adventure began at a time when the Soviet Union was fast moving to its disintegration and the USA had just about commenced playing its role in international affairs as the sole super-power. Secondly, Kuwait was a very small dot on the world map, and still it is, but it is the third or fourth largest producer of oil, hence its significance in global energy demand and supply. Finally, although ever since the British carved out this tiny territory out of the sickman of Europe, the Ottoman empire, it had prospered under their umbrella rather unashamedly. Its ruling family is a kith and kin of its counterpart in Saudi Arabia, the chief supplier of cheap energy to the USA and the west, and its main Arab ally.

Hence, the USA grabbed Saddam's folly primarily to assert its hegemony over the middle-east. Saddam's misadventure lasted for only few weeks, the actual military operations a total of 42 days. A regional dispute could have been contained and resolved with the help from UN and friendly powers. For instance, E. Primakov, then foreign minister of the Soviet Union and a former ambassador to Iraq, made in February 1991 a last minute bid to intervene by formulating a peace proposal after meeting Saddam at Baghdad. But the US did not even allow it to be discussed in the UN Security Council. Instead, it propelled the UN to build up a coalition for military action. Thus began the first Gulf war. On February 29, 1991 US ground forces invaded from Saudi Arabia. An abject defeat of Saddam and his generals followed within 21 days.

Saddam had been by now turned from a friend into a devil incarnate. As the then US president, Bush I explained, the military action against Saddam, that is to say, the first Gulf war, was about access to energy resources and "our way of life".[12] In other words, a self-proclaimed US responsibility in post-cold war world for maintaining a stable regional security environment tuned to its own economic and regional interests.

---

12. As cited in Nasser Aruri, "*America's War Against Iraq*, 1990-2002", in Anthony Arnove, ed. (2002), *op.cit.*, p. 37.

It may therefore appear logical that the first Gulf war was extended in other forms by Clinton and Bush II administrations till the regime-change in Iraq and US rule over it in April 2003. Meanwhile, the people of Iraq somehow endured untold miseries and deprivation for twelve long years. The US aim of, what Noam Chomsky had termed "a Carthaginian solution for Iraq,"[13] that is to say, total destruction of society a'la pre-Christian Carthage, remained unfulfilled.

13. Noam Chomsky, *op.cit.*, p. 70.

6

WE, THE PEOPLE OF IRAQ

About a year before the end of war with Iran, in October 1987, the population of Iraq was 16.34 million, while a decade later, in 1997, it had increased to more than 22 million.[1] In between, Iraq had lost about 240,000 men in its war with Iran, about 58,000—62,000 in first Gulf war,[2] while a couple of thousands died, by US-UK air-raids, UN sanctions and Saddam's coercive regime, let us say, about 3,50,000. Yet, as we can see, the Iraqis continued to multiply.

On the other hand, Iraq's earnings from its oil exports had increased to $ 15.400 million averaging annually about $ 3.1 million (pre-1980) level after war with Iran and by the time first Gulf war commenced in 1991.[3] USA's "Carthaginian" solution of Iraq still was not in sight, though every Iraqi without exception suffered unprecedented misery and unparalleled hardship for twelve long years.

Yet successive US Presidential administrations from Bush I to Bush II never gave up trying; so much so that since July-August 1990 Saddam Husain was turned into a devil incarnate in their estimation.

In the early hours of August 2, 1990, six crack divisions of Iraqi army had entered Kuwait and it had taken over Kuwait city, its capital within four hours. Saddam had claimed the

1. *Regional Surveys of the World: The Middle East and North Africa 2003*, (2003), 49th Edn. London, p. 488.
2. Dilip Hiro (2002), *op.cit.*, p. 39.
3. *Regional Surveys* (2003), *op.cit.*, p. 478.

territory of Kuwait as Iraq's territory taken away from it by imperialist Britain in later half of nineteenth century, and thus beong to him, it was taking back, what was long overdue. But the world outside did not see it that way.

It was the USA that took the lead in restoring the status quo of Iraqi and Kuwait border. Luckily for all concerned, the USA brought UN in picture. On August 6, 1990, the Security Council in a resolution (660) called for a ceasefire and an unconditional withdrawal of Iraqi army from Kuwait. The same day in another resolution (661) it imposed mandatory sanctions and embargo on Iraq and occupied Kuwait. Later, on 29 November, 1990 the Security Council adopted its now famous resolution 678 by 12 votes to 2 (Cuba and Yemen), authorising the use of force for compliance of its earlier resolution on the subject by January 15, 1991.

On August 6, 1990 the USA despatched 40,000 troops to Saudi Arabia after approval of king Fahd of Saudi Arabia was obtained. It had thus begun building up a military coalition, under its control with Britain by its side and with UN mandate.

On 01.00 Greenwich Mean Time (GMT) February 24, 1991, US ground forces entered Iraq from Saudi Arabia. The operation was code named 'Desert Storm.' At 16.30 GMT the same day, in about four and half hours' time UN Security Council was scheduled to consider USSR's peace proposals, but when it did, the USA had summarily rejected these. A day earlier, on February 23 at 12.00 (GMT), Iraq had announced its acceptance of UN call for withdrawal of its forces from Kuwait. On the very next day of US attack, February 25, it had actually ordered withdrawal from Kuwait. By noon on February 26, Iraqi troops withdrew from Kuwait city and its suburbs and a long convoy of Iraqi tanks, armoured personnel carriers, trucks, buses, hijacked cars, etc., was on its way back to Iraqi town of Basra along six-lane Highway 80.

It was this very long convoy of withdrawing 12 divisions, which was hit twenty miles west out of Kuwait at its head and tail by US aircrafts. The convey was stopped and destroyed completely. This slaughter of retreating men and machines continued for next forty hours until temporary truce at 08.00 local time on February 28, 1991. US army, however, continued the killings on the ground, when weather turned unsuitable for aerial bombing. The estimated casualties of Iraqis on the retreat march were about 25000—30000.[4]

The war was very soon brought to Iraqi territory itself. The US military operation had really begun on January 16, 1991 when aerial bombing and cruise missiles were launched from US warships. After 42 days of almost one-sided war, about 65,000 Iraqi's were dead (as against 141 US and 29 British) and about 2000 square miles of Iraq was occupied by the USA and its coalition partners. A specific feature of coalition onslaught was the record of air sorties, 110,000 and 99,000 explosives were dropped, including targets inside Iraq. This count was five to seven times in strength of nuclear bomb dropped on Hiroshima.[5] Fatal casualties apart, such a massive high-tech bombing of Iraq gave a lethal blow to Iraqi infrastructure and civilian installations.

Even after destruction of Iraq's military might and restoration of Kuwait as an Independent state, Bush I administration was not satisfied. The fact that a formal ceasefire was agreed by the coalition and the Iraqi government by early March 1991 was plainly ignored. Broadly speaking, the UN mandate was carried out once the Iraqi aggression was defeated and punished. But the US administration moved on. It was under fire from conservative and Israeli lobbyists in the USA as to why US forces left Saddam to rule in Baghdad. Why did they not take over Baghdad, a feat they could have easily accomplished "in another day and half", as Gen. Sir Peter de La Billiere, the commander of British troops in 'operation desert Storm' claimed in a book, *Storm Command*, published in 1992. Sir Peter explained: "But in pressing on to the Iraqi capital, we would have moved outside the remit of United Nations authority, within which we have worked so far."[6]

In this connection, it is worth our while to recall resolution 687 (the mother of all resolutions) adopted by the UN Security Council on April 3, 1991 by twelve to one (Cuba) and two

---

4. Dilip Hiro, *op.cit.*, p. 39.
5. *Ibid.*
6. As cited in *Ibid.*, p. 40.

absentations (Yemen and Ecquador). This was an important document as it still remains UN mandated framework for dealing with Iraq after the armistice in the first Gulf war.[7] This is a document of thirtyfour paragraphs passed under Chapter VII of the UN Charter, "Action with Respect to Threats to the Peace, Breaches of Peace, and Acts of Aggression". Resolution 687 removed embargo on food, eased restrictions on essential civilian needs (like medicine) and unfroze Iraq's foreign debts. It also provided for deployment of UN military observers in the demilitarized zone along the Iraqi-Kuwait border and only then it provided for the coalition troops to vacate in Southern Iraq. However, the lifting of other embargo, in fact quite extensive, was made contingent on the elimination of Iraq's non-conventional weapons (chemical, biological and missiles beyond a limited range), later came to be known as weapons of mass destruction (WMD) under UN supervision as well as on compensation to victims of Iraqi actions (mainly Kuwaitese and later included were Iraqi Kurds). The resolution certainly implied its acceptance by Iraq in toto but did not include use of force on non-compliance. Iraq accepted the resolution 687 without condition, two days later, on April 6, 1991.

In March 1991, President Bush I did not, however, press forward simply because of lack of UN mandate, although it was still not to be ignored totally in 1990-91. There were other important considerations as well. By defeating Iraq's aggression the USA had then certainly reaffirmed and demonstrated that it remained the dominant force in the middle-east, indeed in the world. This was a message for Israel not to repeat its airstrike on Iraq as well as for the disintegrating USSR not to seek any more compromises for Saddam. Besides, two major US allies in the region, Saudi Arabia and Turkey, were then opposed to it. Turkey, for fear of the enlargement of the power of Kurds in northern Iraq and unrest among its own Kurd nationals. Saudi Arabia, because of fear of destability and civil war in post-Saddam Iraq, near its borders. Finally, the race for a new presidential election had commenced in the USA. President Bush I was reluctant to take unnecessary risks,

7. For the text of resolution 687, See Appendix.

like civil war and destability in Iraq and further US casualties.

So a defeated Saddam with US-UK war planes flying over and killing Iraqis in no-fly zone in north Iraq on the pretext of protecting the Kurds from cruel Saddam—all these were considered, since early autumn 1991, particularly after Soviet disintegration, good enough to keep the Iraqi issue moving the US way. No doubt, UK war planes helped by doing their bit in no fly-zone below 32nd parallel in the south, from August 1992 also on the pretext of protecting the Iraqi shias.

Meanwhile, Saddam had continued on his drive of suppression and coercion against all reasons and logic. Only a few weeks after the first Gulf war armistic, he brutally crushed an uprising of Shias in south Iraq in March 1991. Immediately after, during March-April 1991, he unleashed his crack army divisions on a Kurd rebellion in northern Iraq. These military operations were carried out with the USA and its allies quietly watching. White House spokesman grandiously announced on March 24, 1991 that President Bush had no intention of involving his administration in a civil war in Iraq because "the American people have no stomach for a military operation to dictate the outcome of a political struggle in Iraq".[8]

Surely, the UN adopted its Security Council resolution 686 condemning Iraq's suppression of Shias and Kurds. Also, US war planes, flying from their base at Inciric in Turkey intensified their patrolling of no-fly zone in north Iraq, above 36 parallel. It may be recalled that since October 1991 no-fly zone in the north was meant to protect Kurds while later, since August 1992, no-fly zone in south, below 38 parallel was to protect Shias, though both were self-proclaimed by the USA, UK and France without UN mandate. These high-tech uninterrupted air activities in no-fly zones brought still more havoc and civilian casualties to Iraq through their massive precision missiles and huge explosives. Later recalling earlier air raids, an Iraqi journalist of Baghdad was reported to have noted in her diary-entry for April 15, 1991: "After the war ended, the allies spent all day and all night flying over our

8. *Guardian* (London), March 28, 1991.

heads and breaking sound barrier ... our torture went on for months".[9]

These air raids hardly ever could be blocked by Iraqi radars. But these did not help much President Bush I in getting re-elected in November 1992. Iraq was however, an issue which the Republicans had hoped to reap benefit from. Instead, an unknown Democrat Governor of an obscure southern state, Arkansas, Bill Clinton, to the delight of Saddam Husain and his foreign minister, Tariq Aziz, got elected.

Saddam regime had probably expected a better treatment from the Democrat presidential administration which had, occupied White House in January 1993. How wrong were they, proved later. Little did they understood US presidential election politics and realize that Saddam and his regime had in a way did help Bill Clinton in catapulating to White House.

The new Clinton administration had come to White House with a public commitment of not only continuing the policies of previous administration on Iraq but also intensifying it. The frequency of air surviellence in no-fly zones in north and south Iraq was increased without losing time, hence the devastation of Iraq was also accelerated.

On the other hand, Iraq began to defy frequently, though unsuccessfully, air sorties in the south no-fly zone and the UN itself. On January 1993, it had even refused entry to UN-special commission on disarming Iraq (Unscom). It invited massive retaliation from the very next day by US and UK war planes that devastated in-between the two no-fly zones, Iraq's ground to air missiles and radar sites and tele-communication system, and it caused also considerable civilian casualties. Among others things, the then Iraqi leadership had probably miscalculated US intentions in the period of transition to a new US administration.

The Clinton administration had obviously no intention of slowing down military operations inside Iraq itself and other non-military activities against Iraq. On June 27, 1993, it really got going by launching cruise missiles on Iraq's intelligence headquarters in Baghdad. This was a ferocious and deadly

9. Dilip Hiro (2003), *op.cit.*, p. 47.

attack with high cvilian deaths which included the demise of a prominent Iraqi painter, Leila Attar.

Finally, a pretext, a cause, in fact anything suiting the convenience of the occasion, had become a distinctive feature of US policy towards Iraq. Admittedly, this exercise was deliberately done to influence public opinion and to feed stories to the great American media, but a lot of time and money was spent on explaining alround. President Clinton's first major military action against Iraq this time in June 1993 was publicised as a punishment to Iraq for allegedly plotting to assassinate President Bush during a visit to Kuwait.[10] Iraq immediately denied it but later, the clumsiness of Kuwaiti intelligence proved this allegation really false. As President Clinton's policy of threatening to use force or actually using force unilaterally unfolded, the USA reaffirmed its hegemony over the middle-east. Kuwait was yet another Arab state which now came under direct US protection.

However, two major countries of the region, Iraq and Iran, still posed a challenge for US hegemony in the region. The era of "dual containment" policy of 1980s when both Iraq and Iran were viewed as main challengers to US interests was not yet really over. Only the priority had been reshuffled with Iraq on top of the agenda since Saddam threw a challenge by seeking to create a greater Iraq after forceful annexation of Kuwait. A greater Iraq could become a powerful regional power with known oil reserves, combined with those of Kuwait, more than Saudi Arabia, the largest producer of oil in the world and the chief US ally in the Arab world. Thus a potential threat to US hegemony over the region as well as to yet another US ally, Israel. Besides, it could unleash the fury of the powerful Jewish lobby in the USA itself. Hence Iraq had to be brought under US control and submission by any mean, destruction and war included, with or without UN mandate. These were the objectives of US policy towards Iraq certainly during the decade, 1993-2003.

In a characteristic fashion of US establishment, these

10. Anthony Arnove, ed. (2002), *op.cit.*, p. 3.

objectives in view were claimed as noble and humane. The two-term Clinton administration labelled it differently as it changed its goal posts at various points of time: "To get people of Iraq rid of a tyrant, ruthless, indeed a devil incarnate—Saddam"; "to make Iraq safe for democracy and for prosperity of Iraqi people, the Arabs, indeed for all concerned"; etc. The succeeding Bush II administration was brutally frank: "regime change from Saddam and his Baath party to a mini-USA in the region", "a final solution of security of Israel and the Palestine issue chosen and approved by Israel alone", "the unfinished agenda of first Gulf war of 1991" and "finishing off terrorism post-9/11", etc. This list of name-titles could be easily expanded and made much longer, thanks to official US pronouncements, US and Israeli press, conservative US thinktanks and Israeli lobby.

In pursuit of these objectives, no-hold barred means and methods employed were varied but effective. Diplomacy; bombing out Iraqi infrastructure and men and materials; starving of Iraqi people to submission to US hegemony; and killing of Iraqis by Iraqis themselves through encouraging Kurds, the Shias and emigre Iraqis in the west through help and funding from CIA and friendly Arab powers, like Jordan and Saudi Arabia, and of course, Israel. Finally, a straightforward military occupation by use of force in March 2003.

Such means and methods could be easily documented from reliable US and other non-Arab sources. But two most fatal consequences of these means and methods adopted by the US establishment, stand out; the UNO and international stability, peace and sovereignty, and the untold miseries of Iraq and its people. We certainly look into these two fatal fallbacks in the following pages.

The Clinton administration doggedly pursued the so-called noble and humane objectives in Iraq. At the beginning of his second term in office, President Clinton assured the US public in 1997 that "sanctions (against Iraq) will be there until the end of the time or so long as he (Saddam Husain) lasts". Towards the end of his second term, the prestigious US Journal, *Foreign Affairs*, published an article in its May/June 1999 issue on sanctions on Iraq, and concluded that war against the people of Iraq had resulted in "hundreds of thousands of deaths and more than 140 billion in oil revenues".[11]

The successor administration of President George W. Bush (Bush II) added to this pursuit a marked linkage between its policies towards Iraq and Israel right from the day one. A hawkish conservative US administration with vice-president Dick Cheney, defence secretary Donald Rumsfield, and secretary of state, Collin Powell, the old warriors team of first Gulf war, with an added background of vice-president of being an active lobbyists for Israel and for US oil cartels, had now returned to power. This administration was itching to finish off its agenda of first Gulf war.

The 9/11 2001 unfortunate tragic attack on World Trade Centre in New York's lower Manhattan shocked the world, while it turned the US administration angry and revengeful. The USA once again found an enemy to target. This was Osama bin Laden, a former portégé of CIA in Afghanistan, fighting against the then Soviet troops and a fugitive Saudi millionaire and his tiny band of crazy warriers, *Al Qaeda* or "the base in an organization" (translated in English).

President Bush II launched his war against terrorism, which in his view, was inspired and organised in essence by none others than the Arabs, in particular, and religious fundamentalists among 1.4 billion Muslims of the world, in general. Afghanistan was declared as one *Al Qaeda* main base. By December 2001, it was quickly disposed off, occupied and a chosen government was installed with coalition forces guarding it alround.

Iraq was the next, 'an unfinished agenda' of the first Gulf War. Iraq was certainly never forgotten, as indirect war through UN sanctions, no-fly zones had continued. As a matter of fact, the Gulf War had not ended for the USA and its allies. Now after Afghanistan, President Bush II was ready to bring direct war to Iraq. Preparations for it began in earnest once the President had given green signal. On 29 January 2002 in his

11. *Ibid.*, p. 43.

State of Union message he told the world that North Korea, Iran and Iraq constituted "an axis of evil, arming to threaten the peace of the world". He also made it clear that Iraq was the next goal-post for US war against terrorism. The USA had made up its mind. What needed was to organise the most portent means for disposing off Saddam and Iraq, as quickly as possible. Meanwhile, Israeli army was unleashed by Bush II administration on Arab Palestinians.

The country of Iraq was equated by Bush II administration with Saddam Husain and his Baath party of about 50,000 at the height of his power. As usual, Saddam was absurdly confident and rashly defiant. Iraq was one of the three countries (the other two being Libya and China) who did not fly half-mast at UN New York headquarters in memory of victims of 9/11 destruction. According to London's *Daily Telegraph* of December 22, 2001, the then Iraqi foreign minister Nagi Sabri even publicly reminded America of its "own bloody trail littered with millions of dead going back more than fifty years since the US drop of Atom bomb in Hiroshima in 1945".

If the USA needed a fuel at all in its war against terrorism, such views, publicised from Saddam government apparatus, was surely one. "Target Iraq" was no longer a favourite hobby horse of hawkish Bush II administration but it had now turned into a popular cause of revenge and teaching the Arabs a lesson on US power and global reach. The US media joined the war cry in a big way across the spectrum, encompassing not merely the popular and sensational ones. To give one example. *New York Times* columnist Thomas Friedman, a leading hawk on Iraq during President Clinton administration and later, wrote in his paper as recently as on August 18, 2002: "If the Bush team is serious about Iraq, it needs to zero-in on one clear objective, produce a tightly focused war plan around it and then sell it—with a simple bumper sticker—to America and the world."[12]

Spring and early summer 2002 were spent in military build-

12. Cited in *Ibid.*, p. 22. For a coverage of US media on Iraq, see Ali Abunimah and Rania Masri, *"The Media's Deadly Spin on Iraq"*, in *Ibid.*, pp. 110-13.

up and in convincing US allies across the globe on the inevitability of military action against Saddam's Iraq. None opposed the war but it turned out into an exercise of convincing the non-convinced. Large majority of nations wanted UN model of First Gulf War, only after proven non-compliance by Iraq of Security Council Resolution 687.

The USA pressed particularly its European partners, and not only its faithful supporter, Tony Blair's Britain, to stand by it in regime-change in Iraq by sheer use of brute force. The issue of non-compliance by Iraq of Security Council Resolution 687 was a non-issue for the USA, and it was declared no more relevant. But the issue of weapons of mass destruction (WMD) hidden by Saddam regime was alive, and it had to be dealt with immediately without dilly-dallying. USA's leading European partners, France, Germany and Russia, were still not convinced. Meanwhile, UN Monitoring, Verification and Inspection Commission (UNMOVIC), led by chief UN weapons inspector, Hans Blix, had continued its search in Iraq with a marked cooperation of Iraqi officials for biological and chemical agents and weapons of mass destruction (WMD) inside Iraq. Simultaneously, El-Bradei, chief of Vienna-based International Atomic Energy Agency (IAEA), hunted in Iraq for nuclear weapons and facilities.

Through autumn 2002 and mid-winter 2002-2003, the final scene shifted to UN Security Council meetings. UNMOVIC and IAEA chiefs reported no trace of WMD in Iraq yet, and held up final judgement until more on-the-spot inspections. El-Bradei, however reported a final no, for hidden nuclear weapons and facilities in Iraq.

These reports were debated in UN Security Council meetings in December 19, 2002 and February 2003 in a surcharged atmosphere. No more time given, no more UN meetings on the issue were notified, and no decision was made. In other words, the UN was incapacitated. The line-up was however, clear. The USA and UK did not care for the UN as the decision to wage war against Iraq, was already made by the USA and UK much before the issue of non-compliance by Iraq of Security Council Resolution 687 was brought to Security Council. Their chief European partners, France, Germany and

Russia came out firmly in favour of adherence to Security Council resolution 687, hence more time for UN inspectors for their conclusive judgement as pleaded by them. The "Great Divide" of western nations was crystal clear, though it did not in the least influence the course of events that followed. By November-December 2002, Saddam gave in for still more proactive co-operation with UN inspectors but it came too late.

Once the White House received the final signal from Pentagon, the USA attacked Iraq in full force with Britain acting in consort. Iraq was swiftly occupied by US-UK forces and war was officially declared closed within 26 days in early May 2003. The world was aghast at President Bush II and Tony Blair and UNO was in shambles. But the USA openly and Britain sheepishly were jubilant.

Yet it was obvious that US military was very good in winning a one-sided war but not in managing a vanquished nation. No WMD was yet found, neither was Saddam. US soldiers, however, continued to lose life daily.

At this stage, let us turn to yet another fatal consequence of US-UK policies in Iraq, by looking at the plight of the people of Iraq, about 22 million when US occupation commenced.

We began this chapter by pointing out that the population of Iraq on the last count available (1987) had increased marginally. It survived somehow direct and indirect wars through twelve long years. Direct war, if a one-sided one can be called so, launched by the most powerful nation in history, the USA, was in itself unprecedented and it followed the years of uninterrupted high-tech bombs and precision missiles from US ships and planes. By the end of 1999, for instance, US-UK forces had flown more than 6000 sorties, dropped more than 1800 bombs and about 1500 missiles and these had hit more than 450 targets.[13] In October 1999 the *Wall Street Journal* had noted a dilemma that there were few military targets remaining in Iraq.[14] Pentagon alone spent more than $ 1 billion in maintaining its planes, ships and troops around Iraq.[15] The

---

13. *Ibid.*, p. 17.
14. Cited in *Ibid.*, p. 17.
15. *Ibid.*, p. 16.

frequency of airstrikes kept on increasing and so was the cost. By October 2002, the total cost for the USA was known to have escalated to $12.5 billion. [16] We have no figures available how much UK paid for its own military deployment in consort with the USA.

By September-October 2002, President Bush II had successfully got from the US Congress "necessary authority to proceed immediately against Iraq and for that matter any other nation in the region regardless of subsequent developments and circumstances". It was clear that the USA had gone far ahead in its commitments of using force for bringing Iraq under its rule.

At the beginning of UN General Assembly 57th session, on September 12, 2002 the US President had plainly told in his speech the assembled world representatives that the very legitimacy of the UN would be at stake if it did not act on Iraq the way he wanted. The US President was obviously not satisfied simply by dictating terms to UN programme on Iraq right from its inception, although the programme itself was increasingly being identified in Iraq with US policies towards it.

At this stage, let us look at the UN programme on Iraq. Ever since, the UN imposed unprecedented sanctions on Iraq on August 6, 1990 as a punishment for annexing Kuwait, these had continued in one form or the other for about thirteen years. It was on May 22, 2003, only after US had imposed its rule on Iraq by brute force that UN Security Council could lift its sanctions, with one absentation, Syria. In between the years, there lies the saga of bare survival of about 22 millions of humankind, the people of Iraq from the ravages of contemporary Mongols and Scythians—the men/women who have ruled Washington and London in our days. Democracy and freedom have become convenient choices for the USA, like beauty in the eyes of the beholder. However, the fact of the matter is that US and British establishments of our times had made these great goal-posts of humankind a sham and farce.

---

16. Dilip Hiro (2002), *op.cit.*, p. 215.

This is a discredit to democracy and doubts are raised over its credibility in its current form.[17]

The most sorrowful aspect of this tragedy was the ruthless and cruel punishment forced on Saddam's Iraq as, for one thing, it was quite disproportionate, far exceeding the acceptable norms of laws, to its crime committed and recorded. A 'Carthaginian' solution, a sort of life imprisonment for heinous crimes, was sought against 22 millions of humankind—the people of Iraq—for thirteen long years through direct war and indirect war (sanctions).[18]

These sanctions were put into use through the UN agencies under US hegemony. The story begins when the UN Security Council imposed sanctions on April 3, 1991, through its famous resolution 687. We have pointed out in preceding pages that these were wide-ranging sanctions. The USA pursued these sanctions with its characteristic zeal and US Congress had adopted Iraq-Libya Sanction Act, 1996 for five years. President Bush II extended this act in 2001 to another five years when it was due to expire in August 2001. The USA was thus committed by its own laws, though it perhaps did not require an act of congress, to implement sanctions.

As far as UN was concerned, it decided to slightly ease the sanctions by its oil-for-food scheme, most probably under pressure from France, China and Russia, the three permanent Security Council members. The scheme went into operation in December 1996 under UN supervision. Earlier, during about six years of sanctions, it was claimed in the USA and UN sources that these sanctions were not operated against importing/buying food and medicines for Iraq. But Iraq had exhausted its reserves once its oil exports were totally stopped

---

17. For instance, see, Farid Zakaria (2003), *The Future of Democracy*, New York.
18. For a basic UN sanction document, see appendix. Also, Website of "UN Office of the Iraq Programme", www. un. org. Among a number of useful studies and on the spot personal interviews, we have relied here mainly on collection of articles in Anthony Arnove, ed. (2002), *op.cit.*, pp. 3-5, 77-219 and on Dilip Hiro. (2003), *op.cit.*, chapters 1, 9 and postscript.

under the sanction regime. The elderly and children began to die of starvation and diseases due to growing scarcity of medicine. For a country like Iraq, which, before First Gulf War, imported about ninety percent of its food requirements, this blow was lethal. The sanction was administered by a UN committee, Unscom, at New York, and in practice it was dominated by the USA.

Besides, the complete shutting down of Iraqi oil exports had introduced instability in the prices of oil in global market and it was hurting in a big way the economy of Turkey, a faithful ally of the USA. All these factors led to the adoption of oil-for-food scheme and its operation, beginning in December 1996.

Oil-for-food scheme was essentially meant to ease earlier sanction regime by allowing a limited Iraqi oil export and to use its earnings for buying food and other sanctioned liabilities of Iraq. All these were to be operationalised under Unscom and UN observers in Iraq, and this in practice meant control of USA financially or otherwise. Under the scheme, sanctioned earnings from Iraqi oil were deposited into UN escrow account in Bank of Paris at New York city every six months. After about three years, six-monthly ceiling was raised from $2.1 billion to $5.6 billion and then the ceiling was removed altogether. Out of the sanctioned amount, the Iraqi government received only about half. Out of the other half, the UN deducted 30 percent for the compensation fund for those who suffered due to Iraqi invasion of Kuwait, mostly Kuwaiti nationals, 13 percent for Kurd region which was outside the control of Iraqi government and 7 percent for UN's administrative costs, that is to say, salaries and perks of UN appointed officials stationed in Iraq.[19]

Even this fifty percent share for Iraq was usually controlled and denied by the USA through Unscom on the plea of "dual use" (civilian and military expenditures) under its own smart sanction programme. As of May 2002, the USA was still holding $ 5 billion worth of contracts for Iraq as it suspected dual use of proposed imported goods.[20] Even the distribution of

19. Dilip Hiro (2003), *op.cit.*, p. 4.
20. Anthony Arnove, ed. (2002), *op.cit.*, p. 54.

imported food was done by Iraqi government agencies under specially appointed UN inspectors. The oil-for-food programme was explicitly politicalised with the aim of promoting unrest among Iraqi people against Saddam government.

From January 1991, the Iraqi government had introduced for the first time rationing of food and other hosehold items through its ministry of trade. Only minimum essentials and no meat and fish were supplied. Costing about $5 per capita monthly rations, the Iraqi authorities charged only 24 cents, just to cover the cost. This in practice meant an average 5-member Iraqi family received about $25 a month free ration. Over the years, this supply of bare essential food, free though, kept the Iraqis alive.[21]

But there were acute shortages in other areas of need, like health, education, medicines and vitamin and iron food stuffs. Iraq's share of its earning from sanctioned oil exports was just not enough. Moreover, the way the sanctions were operationalised was cumbersome and problemetic. For each and every item of import, the Iraqi government first had to seek clearance from relevant UN organs, like World Health Organisation, World Food Programme, FAO, etc. Only after this clearance obtained, finally it had to be approved by Unscom. In the process of about fourteen steps to approval, somewhere down the line the request was deliberately scaled down, or approved in instalment or simply delayed.

The end-result was that the people suffered with new social problems, like blackmarketing, thieving, prostitution multiplying every year. For small mercies, the people thanked the Saddam regime, while contrary to expectations, the USA and its publicised concerns for democracy and freedom were resented.

By 2002, it was abundantly clear to Iraqis and many outside that UN oil-for-food programme was never intended to actually ease the humanitarian crisis in Iraq. "It was in fact designed to stop further deterioration.... to build on what the Iraqi

21. See field interviews conducted by Dilip Hiro in Iraq in 2002, *"Life in Iraq,"* in *Ibid.*, pp. 18-19.

government was already doing and is still doing", asserted Dennis J. Halliday, a former top UN civil servant associated with UN programmes in Iraq, in February 1999.[22]

There were of course widespread civilian casualties by malnutrition and destruction of medical care and civic facilities. One reliable estimates in 1999 put "thousands of death per month, a possible total of 1 million to 1.5 million".[23]

As a matter of fact, an entire generation of Iraqis of 1990-2003 lost their prime youth and childhood. For instance, literacy in Iraq fell from 90 to 66 percent. The worst sufferers were children. A UNICEF study in 1997 showed that about a third of Iraqi children were chronologically malnourished, a figure higher than that in Mali or Ghana.[24] By all such counts, deprivations and sufferings increased year by year and multiplied.

However, the US establishment did not relent. Then US secretary of state, Madelien Albright, when told on US national television in May 1996, that 500,000 Iraqi children had died as a result of sanctions, she replied that this (sanction) was "a very hard choice", but "we think that price is worth it".[25] Six years later in October 2002 Arti Fleischer, the White House spokesman in the style of his boss said that "the cost of one bullet the Iraqi people take on themselves is substantially less than that (soaring cost of war preparations-added), and surely less than one-way ticket".[26]

By early summer 2003, when US military occupation of Iraq had commenced, the international system of our times, like Iraq, was in ruins. The world was aghast. Nations across the globe scouted desperately to seek cover and protection for their own perceived national interest. This search a' la Bush II has continued with confusion and disarry of nation-state system itself. The apprehensions of mathematically and US Supreme Court declared defeated 2000 Presidential candidate,

---

22. Anthony Arnove, ed. (2002), *op.cit.*, p. 54.
23. *Ibid.*, p. 63.
24. Cited in Dilip Hiro. (2003), *op.cit.*, p. 6.
25. Cited in Noam Chomsky, *op.cit.*, p. 67.
26. Cited in Dilip Hiro. (2003), *op.cit.*, p. 215.

Al Gore, articulated in the last week of September 2002 in a New York meeting, that "the rule of law will be quickly replaced by the reign of fear .... the notion that there is no law but the discretion of American president",[27] appears to have come true.

Baghdad, the capital-city of Abbasid Caliphs, had a glorious past, perhaps unrivalled in medieval times of world civilization. But all this ended up in 1258 AD, when hordes of Mongols invaded Baghdad and levelled it to the ground. Once again, in 2003, an invading army, mighter than ever before in human history, had invaded and brought ruins to the city, however, less glorious today than the days of Caliphs. But the invading Mongols of medieval times soon left the city and its environment, after accomplishing their mission, to its fate, whatever. But the contemporary Mongol army—the US army—stays put in occupation. Times have obviously changed and so have the modus operandi of invasion and consequent brutalization of vanquished milieu. However, the essence—an indiscriminate deployment of overwhelming superiority in men and materials—was common to both. The question before us, however, is how long will it last and whereto now?

We surely have no answer to this poser in our pages. But the other America, the liberal, democratic and humane America, indeed the entire American people, could surely find an answer. The sooner, the better, for America and rest of the world.

---

27. Reported in *Guardian* (Daily), London, September 24, 2002.

AFTERWORD

Towards the end of April 2003, after about six weeks of unleashing unprecedented military might on Iraq, the commander-in-chief of US forces, President Bush II trimphantly proclaimed victory. Iraq came under the rule of US army, and thus Saddam regime was changed.

However, two proclaimed objectives of this armed invasion namely, getting Saddam and his gang, and unearthing weapons of mass destruction (WMD), were not accomplished. As a matter of fact, the guns never fell silent and precious lives of US citizens are lost everyday. How many Iraqi lives were lost is of no concern to USA. Has the going rate of one US life to native lives gone up since the Vietnam war? Perhaps, not. In any case, the cost of one Iraqi life is even less than the cost of one way ticket to home in Washington buses, according to Ari Fleischer, the White House spokesman on October 1, 2002.

By the end of August 2003, was however abundantly clear that the USA was forcing Iraq not to any kind of democracy, US model or any other, but to anarchy and indiscriminate violence to lower depth by all counts.

Unlike the medieval invading Mongols, the US army stays put in Baghdad. In the latest spin of US policy in Iraq, secretary of state Collin Powell told the United Nations in the beginning of September 2003 that the US forces might be withdrawn "not too soon and not too late". The truth can no longer be camouflaged that US military occupation of Iraq is indeed like the return of imperialism. For the unfortunate people of Iraq, the old and new imperialism have one common basis—coercion, submission and control through the use of massive force or threat to use it. It is hardly a source of satisfaction for them or others that imperialists of today employ different modes and work differently than the old ones. Lest we are dismissed off hand by the "warriors against terrorism" and their auxiliaries, we simply need a close look at Iraq under US army rule. The big game of profiting by the miseries of people, disinherited, devasted and deprived people of Iraq is now in full spin. This is not a small time profiting of East India Company type. Today, unbelievably huge sums of thousands of billion US dollars are programmed for squeezing out by US oil cartels, giant military-service complexes and other hopefuls in the name of reconstruction and 'real' democratization of Iraq. The proverbial dictum, 'you destroy, then rebuild–both ways you derive profit', has become once again true right before our eyes.

In recent weeks, after rejoicing on the return of imperialism to Iraq, US media has shown signs of getting out of their Saddam syndrome. The wild west scenario in occupied Iraq has begun unnerving the great American people; so much so that UN Secretary General Kofi Annan and his highly paid civil servants got busy once more with a renewed resolve in winning Iraqis for the USA, through their so-called humanitarian programmes.

Apart from other important reasons, we have explained earlier, the real push-factor, craftly hidden and effectively confused was the familiar one—Iraqi oil. By the beginning of 2001, the Iraqi oil situation vis-a-vis the USA was the following.

According to official statistics, released by US government Energy Information Administration (EIA), at the end of 2000, US companies had imported an average of 725,000 barrels per day of Iraqi crude oil, 7 percent of total US crude oil imports. Thus Iraq had become the sixth largest source of imported oil for the USA while Saudi Arabia remained in the lead.

This was the picture by the time President Clinton was preparing to leave White House, and even when vice-president Al Gore was alleged to have "crippled domestic oil and gas industries through burdensome environmental regulations".[1]

The inauguration of new Republican administration of George W. Bush in January 2001 was undoubtedly a source of satisfaction for US oil and gas industry, as it had strong ties with the new administration. President Bush II himself was a former head of Texas Oil Company; as president he had begun pursuing a national energy policy that relied heavily on aggressively expanding new sources of oil. Vice-president Dick Cheney, apart from being a Gulf war veteran and a leading figure in Israeli lobby in Washington, was the former CEO of oil services giant, *Halliburton*. National security adviser was a former director of US oil cartel, *Chevron* later, *Chevron-Texaco*. A kind of who's who can be found in top echelons of Bush II administration having close links with US oil and gas industry. The deafening noises of war drummers cleverly camouflaged the fact that in the year 2002, the USA had still drawn Iraqi crude oil, 7 percent of its total oil imports, most of it quietly with the connivance of northern administration of Turkey to beat the UN sanctions.

Not that worlds' largest economy, the USA, could not have lived happily with its habitual affluence and customary prosperity without getting oil from its sixth largest exporter of oil, Iraq, for after all, this amounted to mere 7 percent of its total crude oil imports. Alternate dependable oil exporters were just waiting in the wing through overlordship of OPEC. Besides, faithful and largest US oil supplier, Saudi Arabia with 1.5 million b/d exports to USA in 2002 was always at hand to service, *Al Queda* or not. Moreover, the USA had its own strategic petrol reserves of about 600 million barrels by winter 2002.[2] But why bother at all, when a bigger prize could be easily grabbed without even asking.

The prize, Iraq's oil reserves, are vast. Indeed they are powerful magnates for global oil companies. Iraq is still sitting on an estimated 112 billion barrels of crude, a pool of oil, some

1. "Black Gold Blue" in *www.worldnet daily. com/article*, November 2000.
2. "Oil, the Other Iraq War", *www.msnbe.com/news/82 4407.asp.*

11 percent of worlds' oil and second only to Saudi Arabia's 264 billion barrels. As a comparison, US oil reserves total about 22 billion barrels and about 600 million barrels of strategic petroleum reserves.[3] On top of it all, Iraqi oil reserves are of the finest quality and much cheaper to extract and process than anywhere else, Alaska to Siberia.

Meanwhile, other competitors were inching towards Iraqi oil space with, in view of powerful US oil lobby, collusion of Saddam, and encouraged by 'humanitarianism' of UN Security Council. Russia's oil giant Lukoil had signed contracts in 1997 to develop Iraq's West Qurna oil field. China's National Petroleum Corporation had bought a 50 percent stock in al-Ahdab oil fields. In 2002, France's Totalfina Elf had begun negotiations for similar projects. However, these projects could not be implemented because of UN sanctions.

US oil cartels and construction companies faced more complications than others not simply because of UN sanctions, but the US laws had also barred US companies to deal directly with Saddam government even if it invited them. Hence, both sanctions and US laws had to go and this was deemed possible only after Saddam was disposed of and a regime change was accomplished.

Seen in the above perspective, US rule by force was inevitable, even without UN compliance. The US military action took its own logical course.

Now the race for grabbing the war spoils, euphemistically called reconstruction and democratisation of Iraq, had begun. The US companies are already, towards the end of August 2003, leading the race and they are slated to win hands down. Decisive as the lust for Iraqi oil and prospects of cornering the spoils of war has been, the cause and effect of the very process of return of imperialism to Iraq are multi-dimensional, that transcends Iraq itself. We have focused on major ones earlier in these pages, hence we need not repeat them. Suffice here to surmise that US hegemony in the middle-east and access to vast oil resources of the region, and not mere domestic oil consumption, are thus ensured. The return of imperialism to

---

3. *Ibid.*

Iraq is a far-reaching development of global proportions and implications.

How would nations across the globe cope with this no-hold barred raw arrogance of power and the unhindered willingness for putting it in actual use anytime, anywhere. Obviously, they have to learn to survive in the midst of US imperialism of today with peace and dignity. Looks like, however, that we all have to begin anew from where, after the Second World War 19th-20th century colonialism has moved to liquidation.

No system of domination of one nation or group of nations, however powerful and infallible, over other nation or group of nations had survived for a very long period. This is the lesson of history now and for the future, regardless of some, not learning always.

Who in the USA today cares for history? May be some. After all, there is other America, no doubt, a tiny part—humane, just and discerning chasers of money and recognition. This very America, the world has endearingly known and occasionally admired rather grudgingly, ever since its Declaration of Independence. Will it regain its glory?

Appendix

TEXT OF
UN SECURITY COUNCIL RESOLUTION 687 OF 1991*

Following statements by all 15 Council members, the Council adopted resolution 687(1991).

The Security Council

Recalling its resolutions 660 (1990) of 2 August 1990, 661 (1990) of 6 August 1990, 662 (1990) of 9 August 1990, 664 (1990) of 18 August 1990, 665 (1990) of 25 August 1990, 666 (1990) of 13 September 1990, 667 (1990) of 16 September 1990, 669 (1990) of 24 September 1990, 670 (1990) of 25 September 1990, 674 (1990) of 29 October 1990, 677 (1990) of 28 November 1990, 678 (1990) of 29 November 1990; and 686 (1991) of 2 March 1991,

Welcoming the restoration of Kuwait of its sovereignty, independence and territorial integrity and the return of its legitimate Government.

Affirming the commitment of all Member States to the sovereignty, territorial integrity and political independence of Kuwait and Iraq and noting the intention expressed by the Member States cooperating with Kuwait under paragraph 2 of resolution 678(1990) to bring their military presence in Iraq to an end as soon as possible consistent with paragraph 8 of

---

**Source : Yearbook of the United Nations 1991*(1992), Martin Nijtoff Publishers, New York, pp. 172-75.

resolution 686(1991).

Conscious of the need to take the following measures acting under Chapter VII of the Charter,

1. *Affirms* all thirteen resolutions noted above, except as expressly changed below to achieve the goals of this resolution, including a formal cease-fire;

A

2. *Demands* that Iraq and Kuwait respect the inviolability of the international boundary and the allocation of islands set out in the "Agreed Minutes between the State of Kuwait and the Republic of Iraq regarding the restoration of friendly relations, recognition and related matters", signed by them in the exercise of their sovereignty at Baghdad on 4 October 1963 and registered with the United Nations and published in the United Nations *Treaty Series;*
3. *Calls Upon* the Secretary-General to lend his assistance to make arrangements with Iraq and Kuwait to demarcate the boundary between Iraq and Kuwait, drawing on appropriate material, including the map transmitted by Security Council within one month;
4. *Decides* to guarantee the inviolability of the above-mentioned international boundary and to take, as appropriate, all necessary measures to that end in accordance with the Charter of the United Nations;

B

5. *Requests* the Secretary-General, after consulting with Iraq and Kuwait, to submit within three days to the Security Council for its approval a plan for the immediate deployment of a United Nations observer unit to monitor the Khawr Abd Allah and a demilitarized zone, which is hereby established, extending ten Kilometres into Iraq and five Kilometres into Kuwait from the boundary referred to in the "Agreed Minutes between the State of

Kuwait and the Republic of Iraq regarding the restoration of friendly relations, recognition and related matters," to deter violations of the boundary through its presence in and surveillance of the demilitarized zone; and to observe any hostile or potentially hostile action mounted from the territory of one State into the other, and also requests the Secretary General to report regularly to the Council on the operations of the unit, and immediately if there are serious violations of the zone or potential threats to peace;

6. *Notes* that as soon as the Secretary-General notifies the Security Council of the completion of the deployment of the United Nations observer unit, the conditions will be established for the Member States cooperating with Kuwait in accordance with resolution 678(1990) to bring their military presence in Iraq to an end consistent with resolution 686(1991);

C

7. *Invites* Iraq to reaffirm unconditionally its obligations under the Protocol for the Prohibition of the Use in War of Asphyxiating, Poisonous or other Gases, and of Bacteriological Methods of Warfare and to ratify the Convention on the Prohibition of the Development, Production and Stockpiling of Bacteriological (Biological) and Toxin Weapons and on their Destruction;
8. *Decides* that Iraq shall unconditionally accept the destruction, removal or rendering harmless, under international supervision, of:
   (*a*) All chemical and biological weapons and all stocks of agents and all related sub-systems and components and all research, development, support and manufacturing facilities;
   (*b*) All ballistic missiles with a range greater than 150 kilometres and related major parts and repair and production facilities.
9. *Decides also*, for the implementation of paragraph 8

above, the following:

(a) Iraq shall submit to the Secretary-General, within fifteen days of the adoption of the present resolution, a declaration of the locations, amounts and types of all items specified in paragraph 8 and agree to urgent, onsite inspection as specified below;

(b) The Secretary-General, in consultation with the appropriate Government and, where appropriate, with the Director-General of the World Health Organization, within forty-five days of the passage of the present resolution, shall develop and submit to the Council for approval, a plan calling for the completion of the following acts within forty-five days of such approval:

(i) The forming of a special Commission, which shall carry out immediate on-site inspection of Iraq's biological, chemical and missile capabilities, based on Iraq's declarations and the designation of any additional locations by the Special Commission itself;

(ii) The yielding by Iraq of possession to the Special Commission for destruction, removal or rendering harmless, taking into account the requirements of public safety, of all items specified under paragraph 8*(a)* above, including items at the additional locations designated by the Special Commission under paragraph 9*(b) (i)* above and the destruction by Iraq, under the supervision of the Special; Commission, of all its missile capabilities, including launchers, as specified under paragraph 8 *(b)* above;

(iii) The provision by the Special Commission of the assistance and co-operation to the Director-General of the International Atomic Energy Agency required in paragraphs 12 and 13 below;

10. *Decides Further* that Iraq shall unconditionally undertake not to use, develop, construct or acquire any of the items specified in paragraphs 8 and 9 above and requests the Secretary-General, in consultation with the Special Commission, to develop a plan for the future ongoing monitoring and verification of Iraq's compliance with the present paragraph, to be submitted to the Security Council for approval within one hundred and twenty days of the passage of the present resolution;

11. *Invites* Iraq to reaffirm unconditionally its obligations under the Treaty on the Non-Proliferation of Nuclear Weapons;

12. *Decides* that Iraq shall unconditionally agree not to acquire or develop nuclear weapons or nuclear-weapons-usable material or any subsystems or components or any research, development, support or manufacturing facilities related to the above; to submit to the Secretary General and the Director General of the International Atomic Energy Agency within fifteen days of the adoption of the present resolution a declaration of the locations, amounts and types of all items specified above; to place all of its nuclear-weapons-usable materials under the exclusive control, for custody and removal, of the International Atomic Energy Agency, with the assistance and co-operation of the Special Commission as provided in paragraph 9*(b)* above; to accept, in accordance with the arrangements provided for in paragraph 13 below, urgent on-site inspection and the destruction, removal or rendering harmless as appropriate of all items specified above; and to accept the plan discussed in paragraph 13 below for the future ongoing monitoring and verification of its compliance with these undertakings;

13. *Requests* the Director-General of the International Atomic Energy Agency through the Secretary-General, with the assistance and co-operation of the Special Commission as provided for in the plan of the Secretary-General in paragraph 9*(b)* above, to carry out immediate on-site

inspection of Iraq's nuclear capabilities based on Iraq's declarations and the designation of any additional locations by the Special Commission; to develop a plan for submission to the Security Council within forty-five days calling for the destruction, removal or rendering harmless as appropriate of all items listed in paragraph 12 above; to carry out the plan within forty-five days following approval by the Council; and to develop a plan, taking into account the rights and obligations of Iraq under the Treaty on the Non-Proliferation of Nuclear Weapons, for the future ongoing monitoring and verification of Iraq's compliance with paragraph 12 above, including an inventory of all nuclear material in Iraq subject to the Agency's verification and inspections to confirm that the Agency's safeguards cover all relevant nuclear activities in Iraq, to be submitted to the Council for approval within one hundred and twenty days of the passage of the present resolution.

14. *Notes* that the actions to be taken by Iraq in paragraphs 8, 9, 10, 11, 12 and 13 above represent steps towards the goal of establishing in the Middle-East a zone free from weapons of mass destruction and all missiles for their delivery and the objective of a global ban on chemical weapons;

D

15. *Requests* the Secretary-General to report to the Security Council on the steps taken to facilitate the return of all Kuwaiti property seized by Iraq, including a list of any property that Kuwait claims has not been returned or which has not been returned intact;

E

16. *Reaffirms* that Iraq, without prejudice to the debts and obligations of Iraq arising prior to 2 August 1990, which will be addressed through the normal mechanisms, is

liable under international law for any direct loss, damage, including environmental damage and the depletion of natural resources or injury to foreign Governments, nationals and corporations as a result of Iraq's unlawful invasion and occupation of Kuwait;

17. *Decides* that all Iraqi statements made since 2 August 1990 repudiating its foreign debt are null and void, and demands that Iraq adhere scrupulously to all of its obligations concerning servicing and repayments of its foreign debt;
18. *Decides also* to create a fund to pay compensation for claims that fall within paragraph 16 above and to establish a commission that will administer the fund;
19. *Directs* the Secretary-General to develop and present to the Security Council for decision, not later than thirty days following the adoption of the present resolution, recommendations for the fund to meet the requirement for the payment of claims established in accordance with paragraph 18 above and for a programme to implement the decisions in paragraphs 16, 17 and 18 above, including: administration of the fund; mechanisms for determining the appropriate level of Iraq's contribution to the fund based on a percentage of the value of the exports of petroleum and petroleum products from Iraq not to exceed a figure to be suggested to the Council by the Secretary-General, taking into account the requirements of the people of Iraq, Iraq's payment capacity as assessed in conjunction with the international financial institutions taking into consideration external debt service, and the needs of the Iraqi economy; arrangements for ensuring that payments are made to the fund; the process by which funds will be allocated and claims paid; appropriate procedures for evaluating losses, listing claims and verifying their validity and resolving disputed claims in respect of Iraq's liability as specified in paragraph 16 above; and the composition of the commission designated above;

F

20. *Decides*, effective immediately, that the prohibitions against the sale or supply to Iraq of commodities or products, other than medicine and health supplies, and prohibitions against financial transactions related thereto contained in resolution 661(1990) shall not apply to foodstuffs notified to the Security Council Committee established by resolution 661(1990) concerning the situation between Iraq and Kuwait or, with the approval of that Committee, under the simplified and accelerated "no objection" procedure; to materials and supplies for essential civilian needs as identified in the report to the Secretary-General dated 20 March 1991, and in any further findings of humanitarian need by the Committee;

21. *Decides* to review the provisions of paragraph 20 above every sixty days in the light of the policies and practices of the Government of Iraq, including the implementation of all relevant resolutions of the Security Council, for the purpose of determining whether to reduce or lift the prohibitions referred to therein;

22. *Decides* that, upon the approval by the Security Council of the programme called for in paragraph 19 above and upon Council agreement that Iraq has completed all actions contemplated in paragraphs 8, 9, 10, 11, 12, and 13 above, the prohibitions against the import of commodities and products originating in Iraq and the prohibitions against financial transactions related thereto contained in resolution 661(1990) shall have no further force or effect;

23. *Decides also* that, pending action by the Security Council under paragraph 22 above, the Security Council Committee established by resolution 661(1990) shall be empowered to approve when required to assure adequate financial resources on the part of Iraq to carry out the activities under paragraph 20 above, exceptions to the prohibition against the import of commodities

and products originating in Iraq;

24. *Decides further* that, in accordance with resolution 661(1990) and subsequent related resolutions and until a further decision is taken by the Security Council, all States shall continue to prevent the sale or supply, or the promotion or facilitation of such sale or supply, to Iraq by their nationals, or from their territories or using their flag vessels or aircraft, of:
    (a) Arms and related *material* of all types, specifically including the scale or transfer through other means of all forms of conventional military equipment, including for paramilitary forces, and spare parts and components and their means of production for such equipment;
    (b) Items specified and defined in paragraphs 8 and 12 above not otherwise covered above;
    (c) Technology under licensing or other transfer arrangements used in the production, utilization or stockpiling of items specified in sub-paragraphs *(a)* and *(b)* above;
    (d) Personnel or materials for training or technical support services relating to the design, development, manufacture, use, maintenance or support of items specified in sub-paragraphs *(a)* and *(b)* above;
25. *Calls upon* all States and international organizations to act strictly in accordance with paragraph 24 above, notwithstanding the existence of any contracts, agreements, licences or any other arrangements;
26. *Requests* the Secretary-General, in consultation with appropriate Governments, to develop within sixty days, for the approval of the Security Council guidelines to facilitate full international implementation of paragraphs 24 and 25 above and paragraph 27 below, and to make them available to all States and to establish a procedure for updating these guidelines periodically;
27. *Calls upon* all States to maintain such national controls

and procedures and to take such other actions consistent with the guidelines to be established by the Security Council under paragraph 26 above as may be necessary to ensure compliance with the terms of paragraph 24 above, and calls upon international organizations to take all appropriate steps to assist in ensuring such full compliance;

28. *Agrees* to review its decisions in paragraphs 22, 23, 24 and 25 above, except for the items specified and defined in paragraphs 8 and 12 above, on a regular basis and in any case one hundred and twenty days following the adoption of the present resolution, taking into account Iraq's compliance with the resolution and general progress towards the control of armaments in the region;

29. *Decides* that all States, including Iraq, shall take the necessary measures to ensure that no claim shall lie at the instance of the Government of Iraq, or of any person or body in Iraq, or of any person claiming through or for the benefit of any such person or body, in connection with any contract or other transaction where its performance was affected by reason of the measures taken by the Security Council in resolution 661(1990) and related resolutions;

G

30. *Decides* that, in furtherance of its commitment to facilitate the repatriation of all Kuwaiti and third State nationals, Iraq shall extend all necessary cooperation to the International Committee of the Red Cross, providing lists of such persons, facilitating the access of the International Committee to all such persons wherever located or detained and facilitating the search by the International Committee for those Kuwaiti and third-State nationals still unaccounted for;

31. *Invites* the International Committee of the Red Cross to keep the Secretary-General apprised as appropriate of all activities undertaken in connection with facilitating

the repatriation or return or all Kuwaiti and third-State nationals or their remains present in Iraq on or after 2 August 1990;

H

32. *Requires* Iraq to inform the Security Council that it will not commit or support any act of international terrorism or allow any organization directed towards commission of such acts to operated within its territory and to condemn unequivocally and renounce all acts, methods and practices of terrorism;

I

33. *Declares* that, upon official notification by Iraq to the Secretary-General and to the Security Council of its acceptance of the provisions above, a formal ceasefire is effective between Iraq and Kuwait and the Member States cooperating with Kuwait in accordance with resolution 678(1990).
34. *Decides* to remain seized of the matter and to take such further steps as may be required for the implementation of the present resolution and to secure peace and security in the area.

Security Council *Resolution* 687(1991)

3 April 1991 Meeting 2981 12-1-2

6 nation draft (S/22430 & Corr.1).

Sponsors: Belgium, France, Romania, United Kingdom, United States, Zaire.

Vote in Council as follows:

In Favour: Austria, Belgium, China, Cote d'Ivoire, France, India, Romania, USSR, United Kingdom, United States, Zaire, Zimbabwe.

Against: Cuba.

Abstaining: Ecuedor, Yemen.

RESOURCE READINGS

Angelo Colleoni. *US Intervention: A Brief History* (1984), Indian Revised Edition, New Delhi, Sterling.

Anthony Arnove (ed.). *Iraq Under Seige: The Deadly Impact of Sanctions and War* (2002), Updated Edition, New Delhi, Viva Books Private Limited.

Bernard Lewis. *The Middle East: A Brief History of the Last 2000 Years* (1997), New York, First Touchstone Edition.

BBC (London). *Website, www.news.co.uk/2002/conflict with Iraq.*

Cantwell Smith Wilfred. *Islam in Modern History* (1977), Princeton, NJ, Princeton University Press.

Cockburn, Andrew and Cockburn, Patrick. *Out of Ashes: The Ressurection of Saddam Husain* (1999), New York, Harper and Collins.

Esposito, John L. *The Islamic Threat: Myth or Reality?* (1995), New York, Oxford University Press.

Frank Furedi. *Colonial Wars and Politics of Third World Nationalism* (1994), London, I.B. Tauris.

Halliday, Fred., *Arabia Without Sultans* (1975), London, Penguin.

Hiro, Dilip. *Iraq, A Report from the Inside* (2003), London, Granta Publications.

Khadduri, Majid. *Socialist Iraq: A Study in Iraqi Politics Since 1968* (1978), Washington, Middle East Institute.

Marion Farouk-Sluglett and Peter Sluglett. *Iraq Since 1958, From Revolution to Dictatorship* (1987), London, KPI Limited.

Middle East and North Africa: Regional Surveys of the World 2003 (2003), London, Europa Publications.

OPEC Bulletins (monthly), 1999-2003, Geneva.

Primakov, Y.M. *The Anatomy of the Middle East Conflict* (1979), Moscow, Progress Publishers.

Richard Butler. *Saddam Defiant: The Threat of Weapons of Mass Destruction and the Crisis of Global Security,* (1999) Washington D.C., Public Affairs.

Robert Lacy. *The Kingdom* (1982), Fontana Paperbacks, U.K.

Toynbee, Arnold J. *The Islamic World Since the Peace Settlement: Survey of International Affairs, 1925,* Vol. 1 (1927), London, Oxford University Press.

UN Website. *UN Office of the Iraqi Programme, www.un.org*

William Roger Louis. *The British Empire in the Middle East, 1945-1951* (1984), New York, Oxford University Press.

INDEX